Austin Brothers Publishing

Dear Reader,

Recently I came across a marvelous collection of notes and essays that capture the astonishing perspective of a real-life, modern-day explorer. At times, I found the vivid reflections of Stephen Wesley Dyer to be like reading the crumpled and stained pages of a private diary gone round the world. These "passages" artfully intertwine amazing global experiences and firsthand field observations with the ageless truth and inspiration of the Bible.

I was riveted upon my first reading and felt I needed to bring it into public awareness. Every time our Austin Brothers Publishing team reviews this manuscript, we are ever more persuaded that anyone can find great wealth in Stevie's discoveries and revelations. *Secret Passages of Stevie the Guide* is about life, missions, the world, and the Lord. But ultimately I think you will find it is actually a book about you.

Open this book to any chapter, but cancel your appointments today. It will be hard to put down. You'll laugh. You'll cry. You'll kiss a few bucks goodbye. And when you're done, you'll be asking yourself one persistent question: What's my mission?

So now the first portion of the collection, very much in its original condition and flavor, *Secret Passages of Stevie the Guide*. It is our joy to hand it to you. Get ready to go somewhere.

Terry Austin
Publisher

www.austinbrotherspublishing.com
wterrya@gmail.com

Austin Brothers
Publishing

TRASKIA

CORVS

FAVONIVS

AFRICVS

LIBONOTVS

EVROPA

AFRICA

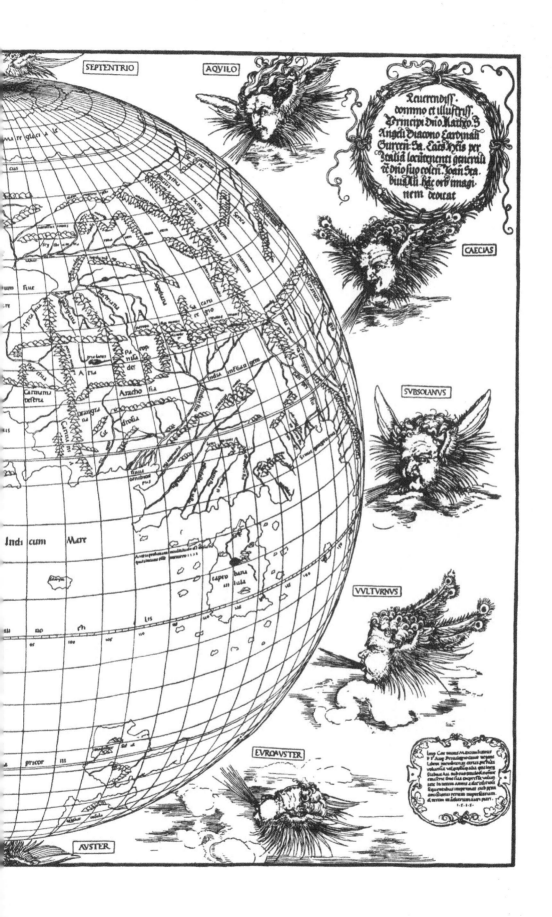

SECRET PASSAGES

OF
STEVIE THE
GUIDE

How

Ordinary People

DISCOVER

An Extraordinary Life

(no matter where You came from)

BY STEPHEN W. DYER

Austin Brothers Publishing
Fort Worth, Texas

Secret Passages
of Stevie the Guide
How Ordinary People Discover An Extraordinary Life
(no matter where you came from)

Austin Brothers Publishing
3616 Sutter Court
Ft. Worth, Texas 76137
wterrya@gmail.com, www.austinbrotherspublishing.com

Ordering Information
To order additional copies call 713-628-1610
Email: stevie3249@gmail.com
or visit www.DyerFamilyMissions.com.
Quantity Discounts are available.
ISBN: 978-0-9891027-8-0

The author may be contacted at the following address:

Stephen W. Dyer, 2261 Northpark Dr. #314, Kingwood, Texas 77339

www.DyerFamilyMissions.com

Special Thanks
Cover & Design Supervision: JoeCavazos.com
Illustrations: Todd Tuttle
ARTOFTODDTUTTLE@GMAIL.COM
Developmental Editor: Hart Simpson
Editors: Karen Pickering & Christy Elkins
Proof Readers: Hugh Poland, Don Holland, Mark Witherspoon,
Sean McKean, Allen Bishop & Edwin H. Dyer Jr.

The Eight Universal Struggles of Missions Discovery and Execution
(Furnaces Through Which All Missions Are Fired and Refined)

GUIDANCE OF THE SPIRIT is the key ingredient of all missions. The Holy Spirit has been the navigating compass behind all Christian action. He is the best guide, not you.

HOPE AND FAITH can be confused for one another. If all you do is cling to hope with your best willpower and intentions, it won't get you nearly as far as hope and faith together.

VISION DETECTION is an art worth practicing. That's the ability to look clearly at your education, relationships, and experiences, good or bad, to gain a vision for your God-given mission today. He put you through it and expects you to use it.

PAST AND FUTURE are not equals. Who you were yesterday is not who you will be tomorrow. The past is only a collection of mission training exercises and directional signposts. You are here with your gear now. This is not a drill.

MISSION CONTROL does not ultimately reside with you. Training, logistics, and target objectives are important, but they will change by the moment during live operations in the field. Get ready. If you want to make God laugh, just tell Him your plans.

TEAM AND VISION are intertwined. If you want a strong team, you must cast a strong vision in a wide radius. If you want them to believe it, you must first own it yourself. Act and speak from the heart.

PRIVATE BELIEF is worthless in building the Kingdom. You don't want to come out of the closet with your Christian faith? Hey, we hope you enjoy yourself in there! Our mission is deployed out in the open. You and your gifts will be deeply missed.

IMAGINE NO LIMITS, because there are none. If you can envision something you love to do, no matter how simple or outrageous, you can serve the Lord and the world with it. One way or another. For a short time or long time. Anywhere.

Change the World

"Take a method and try it.
If it fails, admit it frankly and try another.
But above all, try something."

—Franklin D. Roosevelt

Contents

"If you walk through this door, you're walking into a world of trouble. There's no turning back. Do you understand?"

—Officer Jimmy Malone - The Untouchables

I. The Bread Crumb Trail

*Insights into: Gift Evaluation And Utilization * Favorite TV Shows * Predictability Of Your Mission * History Examination * Who Are You Really * Personal Reinvention * Finding Comfort Level * Who You Admire * Key Influences * Initiative * Personality * What You Actually Believe * The Unfolding Path * Unique Qualities * The Poison Of Pride * The Leap Of Faith * And More …*

II. Secret Passages

*Reflections upon: harsh reality * gross misconceptions * the good in bad * snap judgments * real oppression * pitfalls * dangerous friends * time limits * savage encounters * death benefits * the lens we look through * higher authorities * dirty places * intoxication * catastrophe * and a lot more ...*

III. Missions: Why Bother?

*Notions of: compass calibration * why missions * who and what we are * preciousness of life * earthly and eternal wealth * people of key impact * walk* *a crooked line * tick-tock, tick-tock * getting back online * the bends * fear of death * flying without a plane * divine intervention * and a whole bunch more …*

IV. What's My Mission?

*Advice on: our personal design * your unique mission field * the power of presentation * hearing the call* vision casting * overcoming resistance * strength from humility * building a team * finding sanctuary * listening to God * being delighted * the presence of angels * the coolest missions * mentors and partners * certainty of mission* and so much more …*

V. Excuses, Excuses

*Thoughts about: fear versus apathy * in control and out of control * why you're so blessed * running from the Lord * anger management * sinners who succeed * life blueprints * your sterling qualifications * having a clear focus * planning the future * the toxicity of indifference * personal confidence* spiritual attack * and way, way, way more …*

VI. Bubbling Over

*Inspiration from: your Monopoly game * why does it matter * a noble quest * passion * historical figures * the Berlin Wall * our national challenges * Ricky Ricardo * the urgency of the situation * the perils of inaction * the importance of right now * your personal stories * a call to action * and, and ... well, you know*

"And once you live a good story, you get a taste for a kind of meaning in life, and you can't go back to being normal; you can't go back to meaningless scenes stitched together by the forgettable thread of wasted time."

—Donald Miller

INTRODUCTION

"When the old mapmakers got to the edge of the world they used to write, 'Beyond this place there be dragons.'"

—Berkeley Cole - Out of Africa

Christopher Columbus sailed west out of Europe in 1492 and found an incredible "new world." The news exploded like a bombshell upon his return, unleashing an era of exploration and discovery. More than finding a bunch of undeveloped real estate across the sea, Christopher changed the thinking of a whole continent. Before he sailed, people had a multitude of crazy ideas about what might be out there beyond the dangerous horizon. Nobody wanted to venture too far. When he returned from his mission, thousands of people began planning to make the trip. Why?

It's all about perception. We are instinctively afraid of the unknown, and we imagine bad things that must be lurking there. So most often, just to be safe, we don't go.

Short-term or long-term, missionary service can be a step into the unknown, so most often, just to be safe, Christians don't go. Some are truly afraid of getting injured or killed on a mission, but most are not. They're afraid of other things they can't see or predict. Fear of being inconvenienced, not having enough money, getting too deeply involved, not knowing what to do, being out of control, or having poor food and accommodations may come into play. The very idea of being identified as a "missionary" can conjure up all kinds of fears in people. I know about this.

Do you remember the parable of the good Samaritan? Yes, it was very nice of that guy to stop and help the stranger in trouble. But what about the other two guys who passed by and didn't help? Were they bad people? I think not. Rather, like the multitudes passing an accident or crime scene on the busy streets of a big city, they just didn't want to get involved. Too many unknown factors in that equation, so they stayed out of it.

This book is certainly about me, the unusual ways God shaped my life and steered me toward His service. Ultimately, though, this is a book about you: What's your mission, why you need it, and how you can engage. Like me, I hope you will discover God has been secretly preparing you for a unique purpose.

"For I know the plans I have for you," declares the Lord, plans to prosper you and not to harm you, plans to give you hope and a future."
—Jeremiah 29:11

I am an international Christian missions guide. I lead people into the unknown. Today one of the coolest things I get to do is guide folks to a place where God can reveal the unique abilities they can use to serve Him. It is exciting to see ordinary people wake up to the fact that they too can serve the Lord and show His love to others by using their natural gifts and talents, whatever they may be.

God wired me and carefully prepared me with unique experiences, then revealed a mission for which I was well qualified and naturally love to do. Since then it has been an awesome series of events in serving the Lord and the needs of His people.

I never grow tired of it, because it is what I was built for. God knew about me, just like He knows all about you.

My family and I have hosted and guided hundreds of people into missions on international fields as well as at home in the USA. One thing we have observed time and again is that every believer, without exception, has something to offer the Lord's missions effort.

People who get off the couch and actually go on a mission with us may think they're going for one task, only to discover God has something else in mind for them—something for which He has been preparing them and for which they have real talent. Often they don't know the value of their gifts until they actually get in the game, go on a mission, and take their resources out for a spin.

Recently, my friend Mark, who is very passionately involved in African missions, told me that he hadn't wanted to go on his first mission trip. There were too many unknowns about the journey. But he felt a burden and reluctantly went to Tanzania. On a midnight boat to the island of Zanzibar he had a "chance" conversation with an aspiring young pastor who wanted more education. "It was as if the stars lined up at that moment!" Mark exclaimed. "I knew I could help build God's Kingdom by helping this one man go to school. That's something I could do. That's why I was there!" Now they are building a ministry together in Africa.

Take a peek at my bizarre journey, and get to know me … if you dare. Then ask yourself, "If a guy like Stevie can be a missionary for the Lord Jesus Christ, why can't I? What's my mission?" Unlock this door, step through the portal, and enter a world beyond your imagination. At least, it was beyond mine … and I can imagine quite a lot.

Of all the things we do in life, finding our unique role in the Lord's mission is key. ❧

> *Brothers, what we do in life echoes in eternity."*
>
> **—Maximus Decimus Meridius - Gladiator**

"For what it's worth: it's never too late … to be whoever you want to be. There's no time limit, start whenever you want. You can change or stay the same, there are no rules to this thing. We can make the best or the worst of it. I hope you make the best of it. I hope you see things that startle you. I hope you feel things you never felt before. I hope you meet people who have a different point of view. I hope you live a life you're proud of, and if you find that you're not, I hope you have the strength to start all over again."

—The Curious Case of Benjamin Button

Your Eternal Timeline

You are here

PASSAGE I
THE BREAD CRUMB
TRAIL

A Collection of the Scattered Pieces:
How Does God Build Us for Missions?

*"Children are like wet cement. Whatever falls on them makes an
impression."*

—Dr. Haim Ginott

1

THE G650

"Your mission, Jim, should you decide to accept it ..."
—Mission: Impossible

OU'RE DREAMING AND HEAR a knock at the door. It's Oprah Winfrey with some reporters and a big camera crew. She informs you she's producing a new TV show, which is sort of an advanced version of *Extreme Makeover* or *Pimp My Ride*. After a nationwide selection process for an ordinary person to surprise, you have been chosen! You're the one. Congratulations!

The show's called: *Start Her Up Chief.*

You climb into Oprah's long limo all excited, cruise to the nearest international airport with lots of fanfare, and arrive at a huge hangar. Inside there is a brand-new, custom-painted Gulfstream G650, one of the fastest and most technologically advanced private jets in the world. Full throttle on this baby is Mach .925, just under the speed of sound. The current price is $65 million dollars.

And it's yours ... for free.

Here's the catch: No one is allowed to fly it but you. You can't sell it or give it away, so it has very limited value if you can't operate it. You must learn how to fly the plane by yourself, then you can use it however you want. Gas, maintenance, and unlimited instruction are free forever. Get your wings, and you get to be a part of the team that helps others receive free gifts like yours. Think of the possibilities! You could go anywhere!

It is safe to say the average Joe with no flight experience would not be crankin' that bad boy up for a zip over to Singapore that day … or the next. You accept the free gift with a silly grin for the cameras, but you don't have the first clue how to use it properly, or what it's even capable of. The cockpit looks like a video arcade. You don't see an ignition switch with keys hanging out of it. Hmmmm.

Oprah gives you a big hug, wishing you good luck and all the best. She and the press then blow out of that hangar like a hot desert wind, and you are left alone with nothing but a few remote cameras to record your progress for the entire world to see every evening on TV. You are now the program, and what you do, how you use your G650, is all on public display.

If we came to visit you in a year or three, what would we find? Would you be sitting in the same spot where Oprah left you, using the plane as a luxury apartment, not having learned a thing? Or would we find a confident, aspiring pilot with a growing vision who has been reaching new levels of skill and understanding of his mission? How might your life be different if you actually learned how to operate this free gift? What could you do with it?

This is how I looked upon accepting Christ as my personal Savior, getting baptized, and receiving my first Bible. It was an enormous gift on a wonderful day, and I didn't really know what to do with it. But that was okay, because I wasn't supposed to know everything. This was just the beginning. The easy part was saying, "Yes! I'll take it." So I did.

"Wrap it up. I'll take it."

—*The Fabulous Thunderbirds*

Learning to use the Lord's free gift the way He hopes for it to be used…..Ah! That requires life-long learning and practice. It's big, it's powerful, it can go far, it's deeply meaningful, and it can be so much fun! There's nothing quite like flying your own plane, especially one like that.

So, with whatever bag of gifts and experiences we've been given, good or bad, let's learn how to fly, carry out the mission in this vehicle, and serve the One who gave it to us. If you're already a "pilot," there's always room for improvement. ❧

"You will begin to touch heaven, Jonathan, in the moment that you touch the perfect speed. And that isn't flying a thousand miles an hour, or a million, or flying at the speed of light. Because any number is a limit…. Perfect speed, my son, is being there."

—Richard Bach, *Jonathan Livingston Seagull*

2

JUST SAYIN'

"What's your dream, and to what corner of the missions world will it take you?"

—Eleanor Roat

GOD MADE US FOR HIS missions. He knitted us together. He had a unique, specific purpose for making each of us. He knew what He was doing when He did it.

"We are His workmanship"

—Ephesians 2:10

I'm not sure what you think you see in the mirror each morning. I know I have seen many people in mine, good and not so good, depending on how I feel. It really doesn't matter what you think you see. What matters is that one day you look to the Lord and realize you and your experiences are God's special "cake mix." He has deliberately created you with a unique recipe, and He has His own reasons for doing it that way. God has a mission for you to fulfill during the few minutes you are allowed to be here on this earth, and nobody else can do this mission but you.

It's your mission. So wake up and start looking back at the trail for signs of the mission ahead, if you haven't already. They're there, if you will only see. You were made for this, and we don't have much time.

"There is not a moment to be lost."

—Captain Jack Aubrey in Master and Commander: The Far Side of the World

You are not alone. God also made all those who believe in Him members of an enormous family or team called the Body of Christ. The collective resources of time, talent, treasure, creativity, and imagination in your "family" are vast. Your family is rich, and they want to help you carry out your mission, because their work depends on it. Just as lungs draw in oxygen to support the brain and muscles, so do members of the Body of Christ support each other.

You have an important and unique role to play on this team as a valued member of the family. We need you, and we can't do the job completely without you.

"For just as each of us has one body with many members, and these members do not all have the same function, so in Christ we, though many, form one body, and each member belongs to all the others"

—Romans 12:4-5

This is clearly why we are here together: God's mission and all the multitude of functions required for success.

Discovering my role in missions has changed my life and connected me with my amazing family. The quicker you can get to this "Ah-Ha!!" moment in your life, the quicker you can identify your God-given mission and get going. It will all begin to come together at that pivotal point, but you have to look for it prayerfully. ❧

"If you're a Christian and you're still breathing, you're a missionary."

—Don Holland

3

COME AS YOU ARE?

"A journey may be long or short, but it must start at the very spot one finds oneself."

—Jim Stovall, *The Ultimate Gift*

ONE OF MY FAVORITE CHURCHES in the world is The Church at Rock Creek in Little Rock, Arkansas. They have a heart for missionary service that's bigger than Texas, and I have had so much fun working with them and their mission teams. This part of my "family" has been an overwhelming inspiration to me. Their church motto is "Come just as you are."

Are they really sure about that?

I say this because just how I am, just where I've been, just what I've done, just who I've been around, just what I've said, just what I've thought, and just all the good, bad, and ugly that makes up just who I am ... well, not all of it has been exactly what some Christian folks would call godly or biblical. At least not all the time. I wasn't always sure people like that would want people like me, but they did, and most importantly, God did: "Before I formed you in the womb I knew you; before you were born I set you apart; I appointed you as a prophet to the nations" (Jeremiah 1:5).

I was made for this, and you are too, whether you know it yet or not. All of us have an area of expertise God gave us to use for His mission. I just couldn't see mine until ... wait for it ... until it was revealed. Until the mix was complete, the oven timer went off, and God's cake was ready! God uses our past experiences to prepare us for what's ahead.

> *"Our checkered past is not what disqualifies us from missions or excludes us from our family in Christ. This is a dark deception that many believe. Our past is what uniquely prepares us to carry out our God-given role on His Grand Stage. Without each of us, and the stuff we bring, the play is always incomplete."*
>
> **—Stephen W. Dyer**

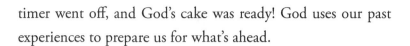

CAKE

"Aye, to the leavening, but here's yet in the word hereafter the kneading, the making of the cake, the heating of the oven, and the baking. Nay, you must stay the cooling, too, or you may chance to burn your mouth."—Shakespeare.

So, the best way I know to get to the part about you and your God-given mission is to first tell you something about me and how I found mine. Let me retrace some of the steps along the bread-crumb trail of my crazy life that led me from a selfish, sinful first half to becoming a (still somewhat selfish and sinful) Christian missionary guide who connects people and ministries in the US to children's ministries abroad. It's been quite a ride, so fasten your seat belt. This is how I am, just as I am, and here I come. ❧

> *I wanna talk about me,*
> *Wanna talk about I,*
> *Wanna talk about number one oh my me my,*
> *What I think, what I like, what I know,*
> *what I want, what I see*
> *I like talkin' about you you you you, usually,*
> *But occasionally I wanna talk about me.*
>
> **—Toby Keith**

4

SEE THE REAL ME

It may be hard for an egg to turn into a bird: it would be a jolly sight harder for it to learn to fly while remaining an egg. We are like eggs at present. And you cannot go on indefinitely being just an ordinary, decent egg.

We must be hatched or go bad.

—C. S. Lewis

MOST OF MY LIFE I was not a Christian guy. I never felt comfortable in church when I was younger. Young Life and Campus Crusade for Christ weren't my deal, and I thought Christians were boring and uncool. If my parents didn't make me go to church, I didn't volunteer for it, and I never read the Bible. I liked to chase girls and drink beer instead.

I have traveled in my work and play, spent time and money doing some unusual things, but I'm nobody special. My friends reading this will nod their heads. Just an old oil field hand from Texas—that's me. I was always adventurous, and as far back as I can remember I was going on missions, but not Christian missions.

If you had told me in the first thirty-five years of my life that the Lord Jesus Christ was carefully weaving together a grand plan to connect me with His enormous family and prepare me to become one of His missionaries, I would have said you were out of your mind. Ridiculous. I would have sized you up as someone with an ulterior motive.

"We don't belong here. It's just not natural. This is all some kind of whacked-out conspiracy."

—Skipper the Penguin - Madagascar

I'm not a pastor or seminary graduate. The truth is I'm no expert Bible scholar either, just a struggling Bible student at best, but I do try. I am an ordinary guy who found a way to use his natural interests and ordinary skills to serve the Lord. Through our immediate family—my wife, Sheri, and our amazing daughters, Ellie and Martha Anne—God has accomplished extraordinary things, because we have turned and allowed Him to guide our lives into missionary service.

He can use you, too. What have you got to share? It may be much more than you think. ⸙

"Each of you should use whatever gift you have received to serve others."

—1 Peter 4:10

5

FIRST INTERNATIONAL MISSION

Indiana: "Too bad the Hovitos don't know you the way I do, Belloq."
Belloq: "Yes, too bad. You could warn them ... if only you spoke Hovitos!"

—Raiders of the Lost Ark

I WAS FOUR YEARS OLD IN Texas Children's Hospital for minor surgery.

I met all kinds of kids in the hospital playroom, and my favorite was the kid from Mexico, who didn't speak any English.

I was fascinated by him and wanted so badly to understand what he said.

I couldn't speak Spanish, but he was my buddy and we communicated anyway.

I could actually interpret for my mom, what he said, even though I didn't know the language.

I could feel what he felt.

I was experiencing my first inter-cultural exchange.

I loved the way it sparked my curiosity and opened my mind.

I was shaped and transformed by the experience.

God was clearly at work in me from the beginning.

Can you look back and see how He has worked to shape you from the beginning? ❧

"I will instruct you and teach you in the way you should go;
I will counsel you and watch over you."

—Psalm 32:8

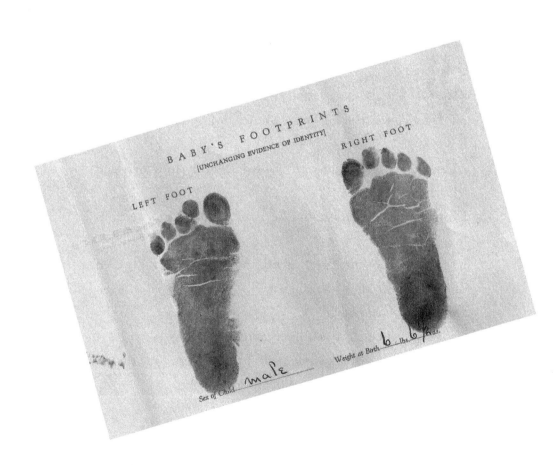

6

STEVIE THE GUIDE

"Twenty years from now you will be more disappointed by the things you didn't do than by the ones you did do. So throw off the bowlines, sail away from the safe harbor. Catch the trade winds in your sails.
Explore. Dream. Discover."
—Mark Twain

WE LIVED IN A NEIGHBORHOOD with a bunch of kids when I was in elementary school. It backed up to a forest I explored regularly. I often packed a "survival" lunch and guided my friends on "missions" into the unknown.

I loved being the guide. It has always been my art form. Everything from maps and planning, to selecting and staging the gear, to informing and preparing the team, to stepping out into the unknown. Expedition is the canvas on which I have always painted, the piano on which I play. I love to take people into "the wild."

"The wild?! You can actually go there?"
—Marty the Zebra - Madagascar

I am also a recording artist ... in my mind. My brother and best friend, Eddie, encouraged me to record the adventure stories I told to our daughters and nieces. So I talked into a microphone about my travels to the far corners of the world. I did small events for schools and shared some of my excitement about the world around us. It was amateurish, but I had a blast! The series was called "The Adventures of Stevie the Guide." The name has stuck with me ever since. It was never a commercial success. Clearly a dismal failure by the economic standards of our world. We blew lots of money on this project. Or did we? Today we see God using the experience in ways we never expected. I still get to be the guide.

Can you look back at something in your life that you always loved, something which can be built upon for your role in missions today? ❧

"I can do all this through him who gives me strength."

—Philippians 4:13

7

MARLIN, JONNY, LLOYD, AND JACQUES

"I could have been a doctor, but there were too many good shows on TV."

—Jason Love

THERE WERE ONLY THREE CHANNELS on TV when I was a kid. Well, four if you counted PBS. The best TV of the week was Sunday night. I never missed it unless my folks dragged me away. There was *Bonanza*, then *The Wonderful World of Disney*. After that, and best of all, was *Mutual of Omaha's Wild Kingdom* with Marlin Perkins. I still get goose bumps thinking of Marlin and all those cool places. Boy, he made me dream! How did Marlin ever get a job like that?

My favorite cartoon by far was from Hanna-Barbera: *Jonny Quest*. The name still gives me chills. Jonny Quest was one of the few cartoons that used real locations and cultures. You could actually look up on a map each place the Quest team went. It was the first time I ever remember hearing words like laser beam, hovercraft, hydrofoil, scuba gear, and jet pack.

The TV show *Sea Hunt* with Lloyd Bridges took underwater adventure to a new level with scuba diving. Later came *The Undersea World of Jacques Cousteau*. These and other shows not only entertained me and appealed to my sense of adventure fantasy, they provided me with concrete examples of people who lived differently. These were people who shaped their lives into something exotic and outrageous. I wanted that.

Can you look back and see things you were attracted to? They are clues to your mission. ✺

"Hey, Dad! Race! Look what I found!"

—Jonny Quest, "Skull and Double Crossbones" (1964)

8

GETTING BURNED

ONE DAY WHEN I WAS about thirteen, my father said something to me that changed my life forever. Dad didn't intend this result, but he lit a bright flame in me that day which never stopped burning. I asked him about my maternal grandfather, Wesley, who died when I was very young. Dad made the comment that the poor guy had gotten "burned" in life.

> *"Momma always had a way of explaining things so I could understand them."*
>
> **—Forrest Gump**

I asked what he meant, and Dad said my grandfather was an honorable guy. He worked hard to care for his family. He loved his wife, paid for the house, and got his little girl, my mom, a quality education and married her off.

Granddaddy Wes planned to retire early at fifty-five. He intended to get a motor home, move to the mountains with his wife and dog, then fly-fish for the rest of his life. He thought he had plenty of time, but my granddaddy dropped dead of a heart attack at fifty-two. He never had time for his fun in the mountains.

> *"In their hearts humans plan their course, but the Lord establishes their steps."*
>
> **—Proverbs 16:9**

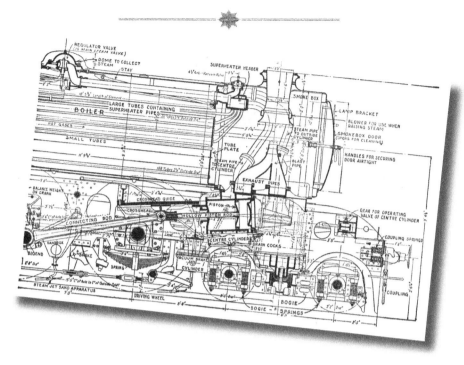

I decided then and there I was not going to get burned. I had seas to sail, mountains to climb, and jungles to explore. I went on dates like other guys but tended to avoid any serious female "entanglements," which represented to me enslavement and death to the dream of expedition. I would not be fooled into getting married, anchored, and hooked to the plow.

My folks took me to Mexico, the Caribbean, and Colorado when I was young, just enough of a glimpse outside my little world in Texas to know I wanted to see more. Much more. I clearly had missions to execute. My kind of missions.

I had Big Dreams. 🎋

"You know what I did before I married? Anything I wanted to."

Henny Youngman

9

SECRET AGENT MAN

I WORKED DURING COLLEGE for Houston-based companies in a specialized field that had adventure written all over it: Global Oil and Gas Exploration. These wild men went everywhere and did everything.

The door to the world swung wide open in 1978, and I was flying around the planet with an oil company. I didn't think about the Lord much at the time, but as I look back I can see His fingerprints all over what I got to do. The global access given to me by oil field work and my God-given fascination with the world allowed me to see and do amazing things. I was so excited at this creation called Earth and its people.

"Southeast Asia Oil Field Trash: If we haven't been there or done it, then we know this ol' boy who has."

—message I found scrawled above a urinal in the restroom of the Cowboy Steakhouse and Bar in Bangkok, Thailand

In my mind, I was Jonny Quest, Marlin Perkins, and Jacques Cousteau all rolled into one. My dreams of exploring the planet were coming true. The world was mine. I lived very selfishly and took all kinds of risk.

"Life is full of risk. You either get out there and take some, or sit at home and watch others do it on TV."

—Jimmy Buffett

I didn't have to call home or tell anyone where I was going. I had no romantic attachments and few responsibilities other than to myself. I liked it that way. It was all about Stevie and his "secret missions."

There's a man who leads a life of danger
To everyone he meets he stays a stranger
With every move he makes, another chance he takes
Odds are he won't live to see tomorrow.
—Johnny Rivers, "Secret Agent Man"

I have always loved the James Bond secret agent image. There was always something amazing about a guy on his own who could slip into friendly or hostile territory, carry out his mission unscathed, save the world, and return safely to base. ❧

"Bond, James Bond."
—Ian Fleming

10

THE GENUINE ARTICLE

$\mathfrak{I}$ WAS ALWAYS INTRIGUED with real secret agent men. Along the way, I read about a little-known military figure whom I have admired ever since. His name was Colonel Andrew Summers Rowan, and he served in the U.S. Army from 1881 to 1909. Rowan was a real "secret agent man" and the subject of a famous story written by journalist Elbert Hubbard.

President William McKinley needed to contact and secure the cooperation of General Calixto García Íñiguez, leader of the Cuban insurrection against Spain. The US needed the general's help from inside Cuba, but no one knew where he was. So this guy Rowan was ordered to go find him and deliver a letter requesting his help. Here's part of Hubbard's celebrated legend:

A Message to Garcia
Elbert Hubbard, 1899

In all this Cuban business there is one man who stands out on the horizon of my memory like Mars at perihelion. When war broke out between Spain and the United States, it was very necessary to communicate quickly with the leader of the Insurgents. Garcia was somewhere in the mountain vastness of Cuba — no one knew where. No mail nor telegraph message could reach him. The President must secure his cooperation, and quickly.

What to do!

Someone said to the President, "There's a fellow by the name of Rowan will find Garcia for you, if anybody can."

Rowan was sent for and given a letter to be delivered to Garcia. How "the fellow by the name of Rowan" took the letter, sealed it up in an oil-skin pouch, strapped it over his heart, in four days landed by night off the coast of Cuba from an open boat, disappeared into the jungle, and in three weeks came out on the other side of the island, having traversed a hostile country on foot, and delivered his letter to Garcia, are things I have no special desire now to tell in detail.

The point I wish to make is this: McKinley gave Rowan a letter to be delivered to Garcia; Rowan took the letter and did not ask, "Where is he at?" By the Eternal! There is a man whose form should be cast in deathless bronze and the statue placed in every college of the land. It is not book-learning young men need, nor instruction about this and that, but a stiffening of the vertebrae which will cause them to be loyal to a trust, to act promptly, concentrate their energies: do the thing—"Carry a message to Garcia!"

This story goes on about employee leadership and responsibility in the workplace. It became incredibly popular and was made into a booklet that sold forty-million copies in thirty-seven languages during the early 1900s. For generations, "Carry a message to Garcia" has been used as a slang expression in business and the military for taking initiative.

Rowan was all kinds of cool. If they had had shaving cream ads back then, Rowan would have been in one. Probably would have gotten his face on a box of Wheaties too!

I always wanted to be the guy who could carry a message to Garcia. ❧

Then I heard the voice of the Lord saying, "Whom shall I send? And who will go for us?" And I said, "Here am I. Send me!"

—Isaiah 6:8

11

WORLD PASSAGES

"Remember what Bilbo used to say: It's a dangerous business, Frodo, going out your door. You step onto the road, and if you don't keep your feet, there's no knowing where you might be swept off to."

—J. R. R. Tolkien

MY FRIEND KENNY RAY once referred to it as "frivolous travel." Dad thought it a waste of time and money. My friend Steve the lawyer once paid me the high compliment of saying he thought I was one of those who had "truly lived."

"Opinions vary."

—Patrick Swayze - Road House

Whatever you might think, I have chosen to invest a lot of my time, talent, and treasure exploring this planet, sometimes with friends, but mostly on my own because I couldn't find anyone to go with me. I just wanted to. God built me that way.

Rather than give you all the sordid details of my purely selfish "secret agent missions," let me just give you a few snapshots of places where the Lord began to show me His creations, shape my heart, and humble me. First, He sent me all over the world on all the missions I could handle. I have:

- Walked Teddy Roosevelt's Badlands
- Flown in helicopters all over the Kenai Peninsula

- Hunted big game in Tanzania
- Watched Whales in the Sea of Cortez
- Visited the Grand Palace in Bangkok
- Worked with scientists on the Great Barrier Reef
- Hiked to the Inca city of Choquequirao
- Descended the Bloody Bay Wall on Little Cayman
- Swam in the Seven Pools of Hana
- Stayed at the Al Bustan Palace in Oman
- Volunteered for Australian Institute of Marine Science
- Explored all the major Mayan ruins
- Explored every inch of Hong Kong and Macao
- Looked down on the Nazca plains
- Held a koala bear in Queensland
- Flown over North Atlantic icebergs
- Observed New York from the Empire State Building
- Watched glow-in-the-dark marine life in the Bering Sea
- Driven across the Mojave Desert
- Wandered Monte Carlo Harbor
- Hiked the Haleakala Crater
- Been robbed in Jamaica
- Spent Christmas in Fiji
- Woken in Chiang Mai
- Witnessed the Aurora Borealis
- Marveled at the Banzai Pipeline
- Lived in the People's Republic of China
- Guided Galápagos dive tours
- Swam at The Baths on Virgin Gorda
- Marveled at Yellowstone and the Tetons
- Sailed the Coral Sea
- Visited the Uluwatu Temple
- Stayed in a hut with Amazon Indians
- Dove to the home of the red-lipped batfish

- Suffered malaria in Colombia
- Visited a mosque in Malaysia
- Survived the North Atlantic rollers
- Skied the Rockies and the Remarkables
- Been stung by a Portuguese man-of-war
- Explored the Pribilof and Aleutian Islands
- Stayed at the Banff Springs Hotel
- Navigated Milford Sound
- Ridden the Blue Train in South Africa
- Ridden on the back of a whale shark
- Hiked in Waimea Canyon
- Ballooned over the Masai Mara
- Viewed the crown jewels in the Tower of London
- Collected seashells in Vanuatu
- Strolled botanical gardens - Singapore and Christchurch
- Hiked the Inca Trail
- Eaten guinea pig, monkey, and crocodile eggs
- Rode a motorcycle all over Bali
- Witnessed a volcanic eruption on Fernandina
- Dove to a sunken ship in New Caledonia
- Toured the tea fields of Sri Lanka
- Slept in Pajom Cave, a Buddhist monastery in Thailand
- Watched the America's Cup in Freemantle
- Explored Old Havana Town

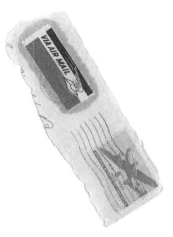

I dreamed of these things, and they became real. God made them happen. I don't tell you this to boast, although it does swell my heart to look at this 55 year list. Rather I choose to share this because it is actually what I see when I look backward at the course of my life. I wandered and explored and marveled at the world. Often I was alone and sometimes I was lost. I learned a lot. As I look at my past experiences I find, imbedded

like the hidden clues on a treasure map, an ever clearer direction to go forward in the Lord's service.

Look back and ask yourself these simple questions: What did I dream about and do early in my life? What was God up to in having me go through all this. What did I learn? What do I enjoy or dream about right now?

Therein you will see the formation of your mission.

"The farther back you can look, the farther forward you are likely to see."

—Winston Churchill

12

THE THRILL OF THE HUNT

DVENTURE WAS AWESOME and beautiful, but believe it or not, I began losing interest. I didn't want to admit to myself that I had reached a point where my missions bored me. I had seen behind the curtain of this idol, and it had lost some of its charm and challenges. My kind of travel was lonely and had no higher purpose other than selfish fun.

General Zaroff: "I was lying in my tent with a splitting headache one night when a terrible thought pushed its way into my mind. Hunting was beginning to bore me! And hunting, remember, had been my life.... Hunting had ceased to be what you call a sporting proposition. It had become too easy. I had to find a new animal to hunt.... It must have courage, cunning, and above all, it must be able to reason."

"But no animal can reason," objected Rainsford.

"My dear fellow," said the general, "there is one that can."

Richard Connell - *The Most Dangerous Game*

This story of the evil General Zaroff is one about hunting men for their destruction. Although missions are about saving rather than destroying, missionaries are hunters and fishers of men, none the less. The biggest game of all, and the stakes couldn't be higher. The prize is not merely their physical bodies, but their very souls!

I discovered the most exciting sport I have ever played. ❧

"The world is made up of two classes—the hunters and the huntees."

—Richard Connell, *The Most Dangerous Game*

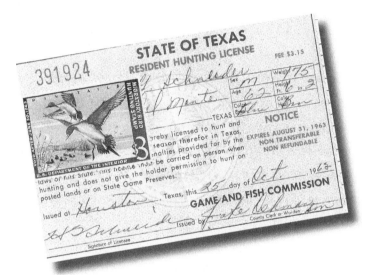

13

THE INTERSECTION OF TV AND REALITY

"Adventure is a path. Real adventure—self-determined, self-motivated, often risky—forces you to have firsthand encounters with the world. The world the way it is, not the way you imagine it. Your body will collide with the earth and you will bear witness. In this way you will be compelled to grapple with the limitless kindness and bottomless cruelty of humankind—and perhaps realize that you yourself are capable of both. This will change you. Nothing will ever again be black-and-white."

—Mark Jenkins - Outside Magazine

I BEGAN TO OBSERVE, as I moved around the planet, that things were not always entirely as I'd seen them on Wild Kingdom and Jonny Quest. They were not as cool as in the James Bond movies. My favorite shows had left out important parts of the real story. The awesome, beautiful sites of the world I saw on TV were always tainted in real life by filthy and horrible things. Always. The ugliness is constantly there if you look for it, regardless of where you are. The trouble is most people are in such a hurry to get to their pretty travel destinations, they only see it in passing, if at all.

Along with the majestic animals of the Masai Mara in Kenya, you get the squalid, sprawling Kibera slums of Nairobi. The ancient temples of Thailand come with the enormous prostitution district of Patpong. The gorgeous waterfalls of Jamaica's Ocho Rios are not far from crime-ridden Kingston. Poverty, corruption, oppression, and slavery come with the territory. El Salvadorans living in homes made of trash bags, Pacific Islanders with no medical care, Peruvians with no clean water. I once saw a man pulling a heavy cart while another man whipped him like a mule. He was literally a beast of burden.

Everywhere I went, there were these children. They wander unsupervised about the towns and along the highways. They perform acrobatic tricks and try to wash your windshield for tips at traffic lights. While they should be in school, they approach tourists offering T-shirts and trinkets, and steal whatever they can get their hands on. Young prostitutes are everywhere, enslaved by a system stacked against them before they were born. These are just the multitudes you can see at a glance. Go into the countryside and you get a whole different look: kids doing farm labor, cooking in restaurants, mixing concrete, planting crops, carrying sacks of grain, tending animals, or just hanging around with no hope of ever going to school.

Gradually, the Lord made it harder for me to see only the beauty I wanted to see on my type of missions. Ignoring what He wanted to show me about His type of missions became impossible. I was shaped from birth to explore all the beautiful things of His world; little did I know He used these desires as a lure.

I noticed the ugly, the unfair, and the unsaved. I didn't know it, but God was preparing me. ❧

"The preparations of the heart in man, and the answer of the tongue, is from the Lord."

—Proverbs 16:1, kjv

14

THE PASSAGE AWAY

MY FAMILY NORMALLY WENT to mass on Sunday. Catholic churches are beautiful and make me feel reverent. I especially like big cathedrals, so big and so quiet. I go into them every chance I get.

Sunday school is where I first learned about God, and I have fond memories. The Catholic Church is where I got the first notion of the Father, Son, and Holy Spirit, heaven, hell, and all that kind of stuff. I'm thankful for that. I know the church customs, traditions, and songs, and I can recite the profession-of-faith prayer. I celebrated my first communion. I know all the basic words and drill of Catholic mass and have attended beautiful services. Sometimes they had guitar mass, which I always enjoyed.

It was not our church or family custom to study the Bible and memorize Scripture. I never saw that book anywhere around our church or home. Today my daughters can quote a lot more Bible Scripture than I can.

My reality is that I grew up Biblically illiterate. I learned about Jesus and the idea of eternal life, but I had a limited understanding of the book through which God can speak to us: the Bible. I was not familiar with the teaching that "man does not live on bread alone, but on every word that comes from the mouth of God" (Matthew 4:4).

We weren't supposed to go up and take communion on Sunday unless we'd been to confession that week. I didn't always tell the priest everything I'd done, especially the really bad parts. I mostly said the penance prayers. If my parents weren't

around, sometimes I skipped confession. I figured I was going to ROAST iM HELL for sure.

El Mariachi: I have to go to church.
Carolina: What for?
El Mariachi: Confess my sins…I'm a sinner.

—Desperado

Mass was often in Latin when I was young. The priests rang bells, did unusual rituals, and swung a smoking brass lantern around on a chain. It all had meaning, but I didn't understand it. I once asked my mother what some of the words meant, like, "Secula, secula, seculo." She shrugged.

By the time I was eighteen, my church attendance had dwindled down to going with my folks at Christmas and Easter. I always believed God was out there somewhere, but we didn't have a very close relationship.

The next twenty years looked like this:
- Graduated high school
- Didn't go to church much
- Explored for oil and gas worldwide
- Graduated from St. Edward's University
- Became a scuba diving instructor
- Sold real estate and went diving
- Found my way back to church. ❧

"A man travels the world over in search of what he needs and returns home to find it."

—George Augustus Moore

15

THE ZIG FACTOR

"If you can dream it, then you can achieve it. You will get all you want in life if you help enough other people get what they want."

—Zig Ziglar

I WAS LURED BACK TO church by Zig Ziglar. I've been a fan since I read his book *See You at the Top*, but his legendary motivational seminars were too expensive for me. I found out I could see him for free at Prestonwood Baptist Church in Dallas, if I went to Sunday school. His class was called the Encouragers. So, even though my Catholic grandmother had told me for years never to go near a Baptist church or the "silly" people within, I went.

It was purely a selfish move to see Zig, but I got a lot more than I could have imagined. Thank God I went. Zig died recently, and I cried my little eyes out. His class meant the world to me. God spoke louder there, or I listened more to His quiet voice along the way. I had always had a fair-weather relationship with God, and never owned or even attempted to read a Bible in earnest until I was thirty-seven years old. Zig changed all that.

If there is one word that describes why I found such joy and passion at this particular church, it would be intimacy. I found very deep, intimate relationships with people there, and God was right in the middle of everything. Men prayed out loud, in public. They shared their hopes, dreams, fears, and challenges. They were real! We studied the Bible and talked about it. I felt connected. When people asked me "How's it going?" they actually wanted an answer.

For the very first time, I felt like part of a church family. I belonged and came inside to shelter after so many years on a long and winding trail. I accepted Christ and was baptized by my friend Neil Jeffries, a former Baylor football player. They called it "being saved," and that's just the way it felt.

What about you? Do you need to come on in out of the rain? ❧

"Desperado, oh, you ain't gettin' no younger
Your pain and your hunger, they're drivin' you home.
And freedom? Oh freedom.
Well, that's just some people talkin'.
Your prison is walkin' through this world all alone."

—The Eagles

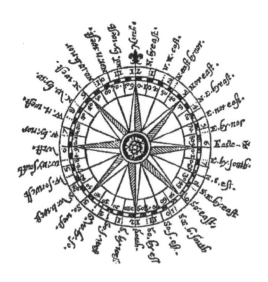

16

THE THEORY OF SUPERNATURAL SELECTION

"I love fools' experiments. I am always making them."
—Charles Darwin

So, I started taking my newfound faith out for a test drive.

The way I have the Bible figured, you either believe it all as God's Word and attempt to live by it, or you don't believe any of it. Period. It is just as simple as that, one way or the other.

Take my cousin Freddy, for example. (Remember, the names have been changed.) I understand him. He's smart, well read, has a PhD, and knows a lot more than I do about history. Freddy's an atheist and makes no bones about it. He believes all the supernatural parts of religion are man-made stories. He will admit there are many true and valuable things in books like the Bible; however, any part that can only be explained by one's faith is fiction. The Bible is not the inspired Word of God, according to Freddy. Although I don't agree with Freddy's assessment, I clearly understand his position. It is cut-and-dried, easy to understand.

My friend Andy, on the other hand, is a more difficult read. When asked directly if he thought the entire Bible was the true Word of God, Andy expressed skepticism. He was, however, quick to point out he firmly believed "the part about Jesus."

Hmmmm … This started a discussion I call "supernatural selection." It went something like this:

"So, Andy, the stories about Jesus are just supernatural stories in the Bible, same as Noah and the ark or Jonah and the
whale. Why do you think the Jesus story is more credible than
the others?" Well, he just believed that part about Jesus. That's
all. I said, "That's about as logical as selectively believing certain
supernatural parts of a fairy tale like "Jack and the Beanstalk."

"You believe," I went on, "Jack actually went

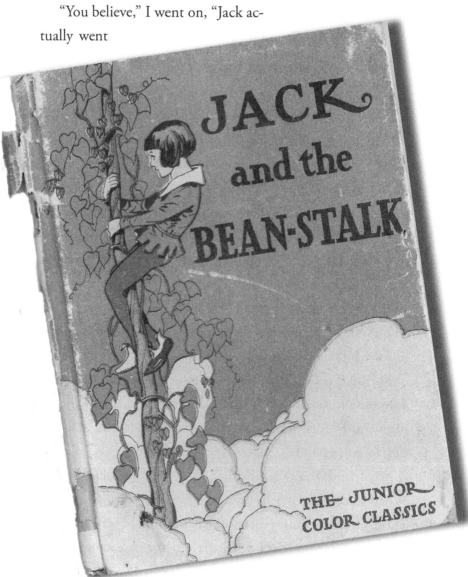

out and sold the family cow for a handful of 'magic' beans. You further believe that after screaming at Jack and slapping him around, his mother threw the beans out the window, whereupon they grew into a giant beanstalk overnight. You even believe the part about Jack climbing the beanstalk and discovering a land up in the clouds.

"However," I continued, "you don't at all believe there was a huge castle, a giant who said 'fee-fi-fo-fum,' a pot of gold, or any of the other stuff. Those parts are ridiculous. Right?" As my Louisiana friend Ronald Dean would say, "Well, that just don't make a lick o' sense."

I've worked Andy pretty hard with my theories and opinions over the years. He has been kind and patient.

I figure the Bible is not a bag of granola. You can't just pick out the best bits and leave the rest. It is an entire body of information, and as I see it, you either believe it all or you don't. It is either the Word of God or it is not. I can't explain it all to you, and I'm not polished at the debate. I have just decided to believe, and this belief helps my life.

"Whether you turn to the right or to the left, your ears will hear a voice behind you, saying, 'This is the way; walk in it.'"
—Isaiah 30:21

And the Bible says we're to be involved in missions … ❧

"If you take missions out of the Bible, you won't have anything left but the covers."
—Nina Gunter

17

WHAT HAPPENED NEXT?

"Blow up your TV, throw away your paper
Move to the country, and build you a home
Plant a little garden, eat a lot of peaches
Try to find Jesus on your own."

—John Prine, "Spanish Pipedream"

o I:

- Moved to the Texas Hill Country and sold real estate.
- Found a little Baptist church and got into a Sunday school class.
- Met a Christian girl, fell in love, got married, and had a family.
- Loved Jesus and being a husband and father.
- Ate a lot of Fredericksburg peaches.

Then:

- Hurricane Mitch struck Honduras, and my class sent me there to help.
- We were introduced to international missions.
- I took my family on short-term mission trips to Mexico.
- We prayed and dreamed of how we could do more.

Then we went on a short-term mission trip to Peru, and the experience changed our lives forever. We:

- Worked at a rural orphanage, school, and clinic.
- Saw that the place was badly mismanaged and going under.
- Met the founder, who was running out of money and asked us to partner with him to solve this growing problem.
- Had an "AH-HA!" moment.
- Saw how our business, management, and sales skills could help.
- Came home with a burden to save this children's ministry.
- Prayed about what to do. ❧

18

THE DOORWAY OF NO RETURN

"There are many talented people who haven't fulfilled their dreams because they over thought it, or they were too cautious, and were unwilling to make the leap of faith."

— James Cameron

LOOKING BACK, I CAN NOW SEE all of the people, places, and situations God orchestrated in my life which led to this critical juncture. We were on a threshold. We couldn't see where it was all going, but God was telling us to trust Him and take … the leap of faith.

To be sure, we inched nervously to the edge of the diving board and studied the water as best we could before jumping through the portal into another world. We learned more about how missionaries are supported by their family, the Body of Christ. We became formally involved with a nonprofit missions sending agency. I got over my pride, wrote a newsletter, and became a public speaker to cast our vision. Support came from some of the most unlikely people and places.

A year later, we leased the house, sold the cars, and had a garage sale. We moved our family to Cuzco, Peru, to manage one orphanage. Our needs were well met by the Lord through our ministry team.

We now work alongside multiple orphanages in Peru, churches in Cuba, and other places. In 2014 we formed DyerFamilyMissions.com. We motivate, guide, and send mission teams.

Swallowing my pride and telling the world I was a mission-ary was the hardest part.

Got pride? **GET RID OF IT!**........ ❧

"Trust in the Lord with all your heart and lean not on your own understanding; in all your ways submit to him, and he will make your paths straight."

—Proverbs 3:5-6

PASSAGE II

SECRET PASSAGES

A Collection of Stuff God Used to Help Me See, Though I Never Wanted Anyone Else to Know

(So Don't Tell Anyone)

"All journeys have secret destinations of which the traveler is unaware."

— **Martin Buber**

19

THE TOTAL TONNAGE

"For nothing is secret that shall not be made manifest; neither anything hid, that shall not be known and come abroad."

Luke 8:17

SECRETS. GOT ANY?

Maybe you did something wrong, or selfish, or maybe it was dangerous, and you didn't want to tell your mother. Perhaps it involved your secret association with someone you wouldn't bring home for dinner. Maybe they weren't bad, just freaky—not your people's kind of people. Maybe they really were bad.

Possibly, you were involved in a situation that was scary or embarrassing. You look back at times like these and realize maybe you just weren't thinking. You have never mentioned it, for whatever reason, and it stayed concealed all your life … up until now.

"And my head I'd be scratchin'
While my thoughts were busy hatchin'
If I only had a brain."

—Harold Arlen and E. Y. Harburg

There are moments in every life that are emblazoned on our memory, etched into our very soul. Issues so confidential we couldn't possibly share them with anyone. The total tonnage can weigh heavily on our little hearts.

God uses these moments, events, people, and problems to get our attention and speak into our lives. That's why when other memories fade, these stay with us vividly.

Many believe these strange associations or sinful, secret scenarios exclude us from our rightful place in Christian life and from our divinely designed mission. I say these fiery human dramas are exactly those required to forge and refine us into shape for our specific mission. Sometimes the refining doesn't feel good, but have you ever seen a blacksmith hammering away at his work? It can be really hot and violent, but look at the piece of metal after it's cooled.

God is the architect and the engineer. He's got a formula for you. ❧

"See it. Feel it. Trust it."

—David L. Cook, *Seven Days in Utopia*

20

THE ZOMBIE

"One flew east, and one flew west, And one flew over the cuckoo's nest."

—Mother Goose rhyme

I WORKED WITH UNITED WAY in Dallas and once organized a tour of a cerebral palsy facility for some of our donors. I encountered a real, live "zombie" in there.

Cerebral palsy affects the way people move, and it occurs differently in each person. Some people have severely impaired motor skills and a difficult time functioning in their daily lives. Others move around and function very well.

We entered the center, where basic to advanced computer skills were taught. Most of the students were moving around, talking to each other, studying the computers, and getting an education. It was easy to see at a glance that each student had some level of cerebral palsy.

I could not help but notice, as I took inventory of each person, one guy in a wheelchair over in the corner by himself. He was sitting in front of a computer but didn't appear to be looking at it. His body shuddered slightly, and he displayed occasional tics and jerks of the head. His thin arms and legs curled up in contorted positions, and his hands were balled tightly as if they had never been opened.

I walked over and said hello. The fellow made no detectable reply, nor any gesture acknowledging my presence. I stepped a little closer and looked at his contorted face. His drooling

mouth hung open, and his eyes flittered around but mostly looked up and to the right. I passed judgment instantly.

Oh yeah, I thought to myself. This poor creature is a goner. Nobody home. Clearly a zombie. I felt sad for him and lucky that I had a bright mind and strong body. I wrote him off completely.

I was about to walk away when I happened to notice a shiny object stuck to the center of this guy's wiggling forehead. It made me think of the gold and silver stars my kindergarten teacher would stick to our heads when we did something good. How cute! They gave him a star. Or did they?

It took me a few seconds to realize the shiny thing on the man's head was not a star at all. I didn't know what it was— some kind of reflective dot. I called one of the staff members over to ask about it, and I'm brought to tears every time I recall what she said: "Oh, this is Stanley, the computer science teacher for this lab. He holds three master's degrees in mathematics and computer engineering from MIT! That dot on his head allows him to operate his computer. See how the cursor of his screen moves with the direction he points his forehead. Stanley is teaching this class right now. All the other students are following him."

I'd been bludgeoned by the chair leg of reality mixed with my profound ignorance. I was secretly as embarrassed and humbled as I had ever been. I was so ashamed of myself. I will never forget Stanley, or who the "zombie" really was that day.

We often say, "You can't judge a book by its cover." But we do, don't we? Who and what have you misjudged lately? ❧

"Stop judging by mere appearances, but instead judge correctly."

John 7:24

21

TIME TRAVEL

"You unlock this door with the key of imagination. Beyond it is another dimension—a dimension not only of sight and sound, but of mind. You're moving into a land of both shadow and substance, of things and ideas. You've just crossed over into the Twilight Zone."

—Rod Serling

A LADY ONCE TOLD ME she had traveled through time. I sold physical therapy equipment for wheelchairs to elderly care facilities and hospitals, and often helped install it myself. This gave me the opportunity to meet all kinds of people from 50 to 104 years old.

One day I entered the room of a woman who was lying flat in bed, face up. She was awake, but though I greeted her warmly, she only stared blankly. I nodded with a knowing smile. She is a fried potato, I thought. Not many marbles rolling around in that bag.

I set about my work, but glanced up a few minutes later and saw the woman was now sitting upright, leaning badly to one side. So, as if it were my mom or dad, I walked over and asked if I could help her into a better position. "Yes, thank you," she mumbled. She drooled from a lopsided face, a clear sign of a stroke.

This is the way we began one of the deepest and most meaningful conversations about the human experience I have ever had with anyone. It was difficult to understand her mumbled whisperings, and at first I felt like making excuses to walk away. But something about her made me want to stay and find out more. I leaned in close to hear her whisper and was spellbound by a wise and once happy woman.

"I like to listen. I have learned a great deal from listening carefully. Most people never listen."

—Ernest Hemingway

Margaret had just turned fifty-four and had lived her adult life way out in the country, the wife of a farmer. She apparently never asked much of her husband, except for one thing: All her married life she had wanted him to build her a bar in their home. For years she had asked for this special feature in the living room to entertain guests. Her husband had always been too busy, and they didn't have the money to go out and buy one. However, this year was different.

Margaret's husband and children gave her the surprise of her life. She came home on her birthday to find a fancy new bar in her living room, and she was ecstatic. Margaret climbed up on one of the four tall bar stools, and her family toasted her with a highball. It was the happiest day of her life. She had the tiger by the tail. And that's the last thing she remembered …

In Margaret's mind, it happened instantaneously: One moment she was on top of the world, enjoying a drink with her family at her new bar. The next she was waking up alone in a strange place among total strangers, in a body that no longer functioned. The first few days she thought it was a dream. "It was as if I had traveled through time!" she exclaimed.

Margaret had been in a coma for four months. A massive stroke had caused her to black out, and the fall from the bar stool injured her head. The family stood vigil at the hospital during the brain surgeries and later moved her to the best long-term care they could afford, but they lived far away and had to go back to work. They were not equipped to care for an invalid, but all promised to visit often.

Life had suddenly turned the page and changed the chapter for Margaret. She had closed her eyes for what seemed only a second, and when she opened them again, her time as an independent, fully functioning person was over. She was deeply bitter and poured it out to me that day. But I noticed a ray of hope as I said good-bye. "Thank you, friend," she said with a faint smile in her eyes. I was glad I had taken the time, for her and for me.

Do you know somebody who needs an ear to whisper into? If not, walk into any nursing home or convalescent care facility and ask the nurses who needs a friend. They'll know, and you'll go home changed, every time! ❧

"There is a time for everything, and a season for every activity under the heavens: a time to be born and a time to die, … a time to tear down and a time to build, a time to weep and a time to laugh, a time to mourn and a time to dance."

—Ecclesiastes 3:1-4

22

THE LUCKY SPERM CLUB

"When you judge another, you do not define them, you define yourself."

—Dr. Wayne Dyer

O YOU SEE THOSE GUYS on the street corners? Their signs used to say, "Will work for food." Usually they wouldn't if you asked them; they just wanted some cash. Later they got more creative and started saying things like "Traveling and need help," "Lost job," or "I used to have a home for my family." A ragged, strung-out guy I saw one time had a sign that read, "Smile! It could be worse! You could be me! Have a blessed day!"

There was a time when I wrote all those guys off as freeloaders and losers, people who would rather beg than work. In my mind, there was something morally flawed and unethical about them. I figured they were on the corner due to their own mistakes and laziness, not because of circumstances. To me it was quite obvious.

Who knows, maybe they were freeloaders, but through what filters did I look at the world that I had so little compassion? I of many privileges. My cousin calls it the "Lucky Sperm Club." I had two educated parents who loved me. They made a fine living and provided a good home in a good part of town. They were not drug addicts and were not mentally ill. My parents fed, clothed, and educated me. They took me to church. My mother was around all day and guided our activities. I had a

good upbringing, and I was given a better chance than most people on this planet. Those are the glasses through which I initially viewed the world around me.

Have you ever seen the movie *Trading Places* with Eddie Murphy and Dan Aykroyd? Two wealthy men, the Duke brothers, debate the age-old question, is it breeding or environment that makes the man? They strike a bet to test their theories at the expense of two men. The impoverished Billy Ray Valentine is enriched and starts to behave like a refined stock investor and captain of industry. The wealthy Louis Winthorpe III is forced into a life of poverty, disgrace, and isolation from society, becoming a drunken criminal wearing rags. It was a funny movie, and I make no judgments about whether any of this would come to pass in the real world. I do; however, think about the terrible fate the Dukes planned for poor Winthorpe in order to test their theory about rich people.

Mortimer: "I suppose you think Winthorpe.....say if he were to lose his job, would resort to holding up people on the streets?"

Randolph: "No, I don't think that would be enough for Winthorpe. We'd have to heap a little more misfortune on those narrow shoulders."

Mortimer: "If he lost his job, and his home, and his fiancee', and his friends. If he were somehow disgraced and arrested by the police...and thrown in jail, even?"

Randolph: "Yes, I'm sure he'd take to crime like a fish to water."

Mortimer: "You'd have to put him in the wrong surroundings, with the worst sort of people. I mean real scum, Randolph."

Think about it. What would it take for you to rob people, or hang around on the street corner and beg strangers for money? Every person has a breaking point. What would be yours?

I once worked with a ministry shelter for homeless men on Harrisburg Street in Houston. It's not a nice part of town. The first day I entered the administrative office I met John, the president, and Jeff, his office manager and CPA. They were both dressed like executives and looked very different from the homeless men who lived in the shelter. John and Jeff were always in the office working together when I came by.

One day John mentioned that he, the president, was the only salaried employee in the ministry. "You mean you and Jeff?" I asked.

John shook his head and knew what was coming. "No, Jeff doesn't receive a salary." The look on my face elicited more explanation. "Jeff is not employed here at the shelter. Jeff is a resident volunteer. He was a homeless person."

I couldn't believe it. This polished, well-spoken exec was living in a filthy homeless shelter with a bunch of drunks and druggies. I was flabbergasted. "What happened?" I sputtered.

John closed the door. "Jeff had a home and family in Tanglewood, a nice part of Houston. He was a CPA at a big firm downtown and belonged to a country club. He had it all going on, drove a big BMW. Life was good.

"Then Jeff discovered **crack cocaine**. It started off as an occasional entertainment, like so many men we see," John continued. "It commenced consuming his life. Bit by bit, he lost the clean criminal record, the job, the house, the toys, the life, and eventually the family and social circle. He wound up here dressed just like you see him today. He works here all week and does a phenomenal job. He's highly educated. On Saturday I give him a token ten dollars for his service. He takes it, goes down to the park and buys a couple of rocks of crack cocaine, gets high for fifteen minutes, and comes back to work another week for us. He's been with us now for eight months."

I looked at life and people differently after that. God has taught me time and again that I have to look deeper.

Jeff was living proof that drug addiction and homelessness can happen to anyone. He was also another example to me that I cannot judge a book by its cover. My heart went out to him and the pain he must have felt in falling so very far.

Whether we are physically or economically challenged at birth, victimized by people or situations in society, or we just trip and fall into a hole, hurt is hurt and need is need—and wouldn't the world be a better place if we all helped each other? One day it could be you. Thank God for the multitude of organizations that help people who need a hand, and missionaries all over the world.

How has God been softening you and the judgments you make of others daily? Has He given you a new pair of glasses through which to see the world? We hear this phrase all the time, but really: What would Jesus do? ❧

> *"For the entire law is fulfilled in keeping this one command: 'Love your neighbor as yourself.'"*
> **—Galatians 5:14**

23

HYSTERICAL

"Sign, sign, everywhere a sign.
Blockin' out the scenery, breakin' my mind.
Do this, don't do that. Can't you read the sign?"
—Five Man Electrical Band

M Y FAVORITE PLACE TO SURF and hang out in Bali, Indonesia, is Uluwatu, a short ride from Losmen Sareg Guesthouse in Kuta Beach. Near this popular surfing spot is Uluwatu Temple, an ancient, vine-covered shrine precariously perched on a sheer cliff face over the ocean. I was fascinated by this place, which resembles a movie set and serves as a high-rise condo for about five dozen furry howler monkeys. These unusual residents often sit like statues for hours and have a regal quality about them. They add drama and mystique to this otherwise creepy, old, mist-shrouded tourist attraction. I thought the temple was cool and visited several times on my way in and out of the surfing area.

One day as I sat on my motorbike out front, five very distinguished and smartly dressed English ladies arrived in a chauffeur-driven van. They approached the main entrance, where a couple of stoic monkeys stood guard along the side, and I heard one of them say, "Oh, Deidra! Please do snap my photograph with this cute little fellow!" She then reached into her tiny handbag and produced a package of Oreo cookies to lure the furry creatures in closer for a cozy wildlife shot.

One of the other ladies called out rather feebly, "Alice, dear, the signs do say not to feed the monkeys."

"Surely a couple of sweets could do no harm," Alice replied. She was clearly enchanted as the monkeys gently came closer and took what she offered them. A couple of other howlers emerged from the bushes, and she smiled warmly toward the cameras as she fed them her last treats.

I knew something was up when I saw two broadly smiling Indonesian groundskeepers elbowing each other in the ribs as they watched Alice and the event they'd obviously witnessed many times before. I saw it coming, and I could have prevented it, but I didn't. I wanted to see what would happen to them.

"Sorry, fellows." Alice spoke gently to the monkeys as if they were a growing group of small English schoolboys who'd appeared on her doorstep at snack time. "I haven't anymore." She wadded up the cookie package and took a step toward the trashcan, whereupon the monkeys began to wail and three of them pounced on her. The four other ladies ran to Alice's aid and were also set upon by a growing number of the bearded creatures who had moved in for their cut of the loot.

The groundskeepers were slapping each other on the back as they snickered, pointed, and jumped up and down. God forgive me, but I laughed so hard I fell backwards off my bike.

There is a vivid picture in my mind of what "hysterical" looks like: those five prim and proper ladies tangling with and screaming at a hoard of savage, howling monkeys that were quickly whipping themselves into a feeding frenzy.

The dust finally settled, and the monkeys scattered when the chauffeur sprinted over and started poking them with an umbrella and waving his raincoat. The ladies were not injured, but a state of trauma and shock was clearly setting in. The bedraggled group was a pitiful sight, and I did feel sorry for them.

All five neatly styled beehive hairdos were in tatters and hung around their shoulders. Two purses were gone to the jungle, their contents strewn across the parking lot. Three elegant shoes, one camera, hairpins, a necklace, and a small brooch had been physically snatched off their bodies. Two of the women lay on the grass crying. I collected a few things, returned them to their destroyed owners, and helped the chauffeur collect what was left of the ladies and their dignity.

Forevermore, I felt guilty for not helping them sooner. Instead, I laughed at their pain. Where did my compassion go? Do you carry the feeling that your mission has sometimes strayed off track? Should you have done something to protect someone, but you stood by and let it happen anyway? ✂

"Not looking to your own interests but each of you to the interests of others."

—Philippians 2:4

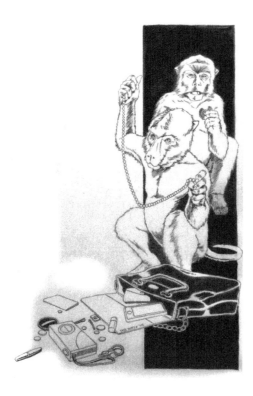

62

24

GOVERNMENTAL RELATIONS

*"A man who carries a cat by the tail learns something he can
learn in no other way."*

—Mark Twain

MY EIGHTH-GRADE CLASS went to Washington, DC,
to become acquainted with our government.
We did.

The group camped at the Sheraton Park Hotel, and by day
we toured the monuments, museums, and official buildings. At
night we stayed in our rooms and played cards. One night my
two buddies and I were losing and quit early. We didn't have
much to do, so we launched into an aerodynamics experiment.
Just some Texas teenage boys who were bored and found a way
to have what seemed like some harmless fun. Looking back, I
wish there had been something more interesting on television.

We got a bucket of ice cubes from the machine down the
hall and started lobbing them out of the open picture windows of our room. Cars driving up the hotel entrance provided
splendid moving targets. The first several passes we missed,
but we calibrated our bearings for drop and distance trajectory from the fifth floor. Then came a line of black cars that
looked like a wedding procession. We all giggled hysterically,
drew back, and fired in unison.

A long limo ground to a halt when the rap-thwap-blap
of ice struck the vehicle with military precision. We laughed
our guts out and slapped each other on the back for expert

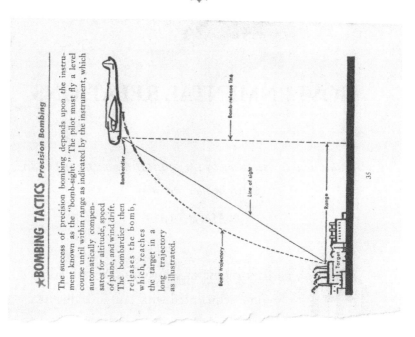

★BOMBING TACTICS *Precision Bombing*

The success of precision bombing depends upon the instrument known as the "bomb-sight." The pilot must fly a level course until within range as indicated by the instrument, which automatically compensates for altitude, speed of plane, and wind drift. The bombardier then releases the bomb, which reaches the target in a long trajectory as illustrated.

marksmanship, but when the entire caravan abruptly halted, we aborted the mission. Lots of men with radios and flashlights exited the vehicles. We quickly closed the curtains and went to bed snickering, thinking our game was over. A few minutes later, the door to our room flew open!

How were we supposed to know that Spiro Agnew, the vice president of the United States of America, was having an event there that evening? We clearly did not get the memo: Don't attack the motorcade, or the Secret Service will be very upset. This was 1973. The Vietnam War was still going on, and a lot of people didn't like the Nixon administration. Within ten minutes, our room was crawling with security men, along with our school officials.

They had the cutest little machine guns.

We were out of bed and up against the wall in our underwear. They were giving us the third degree about how we could wind up in the Leavenworth, Kansas, federal penitentiary. Mr. Agnew had to hit the deck with a couple of agents on top of him when our "grenades" impacted his car. Instead of sending us to prison, however, we got sent home. Leavenworth might not have been so bad compared to the reception that awaited us back in Houston.

This was a pivotal moment in life when I decided my mission had taken a very wrong and ugly turn. I never wanted to do that again. It's like crashing your car. You'll probably recover, but in the future you'll try to drive in a better direction.

Have you ever had a run-in with the federal government? How about with your parents or teachers? ❧

"Let everyone be subject to the governing authorities."

Romans 13:1

Dear Miss Canfield,

I have received your note dated two days ago, the one sent home with Theodore. I have whipped him, his father has whipped him. He is sorry, we are very sorry.
Your friend,
Mrs. Ward Cleaver
Theodor's mother)

—Note forged by Wally for Beaver - Leave It To Beaver

25

SHIPYARD LEGEND

"I've been a wild rover for many a year, and I spent all me money on whiskey and beer."

— "Wild Rover," Irish pub song

THE MacLEAN CLAN SPORTED long flaming-red hair and beards, and proudly spoke the Scottish-accented, curse-laden English of their parents. They worked together as a team in a run-down, junk-filled boatyard on the smelly banks of the Houston Ship Channel. The eldest was Tavish, followed by Blane and Gavin, the baby. They were all in their mid-twenties. Most of the other guys who worked at the shipyard didn't remember their names. The boys were simply referred to as "the Scotchmen" or "the Clan."

Drinking Guinness stout and whiskey, throwing darts in a local pub, and smoking marijuana were their favorite pastimes. They lived together in a condemnable rental house nearby, which was reportedly littered with garbage, bottles, bongs, plastic bags of weed, firearms, and assorted illegal paraphernalia. It was not what you would call a wholesome family environment.

"Stupid is as stupid does."

—Forrest Gump

The Scotchmen worked together on the far side of the shipyard, behind a stretch of abandoned railroad track with a couple of rusted-out tanker cars. They kept pretty much to themselves, doing a highly specialized type of welding for chemical barges. Rarely did anyone go back there to visit. They were all by themselves every day.

The MacLeans' daily custom was to have a half-hour "reefer break" at the ten o'clock whistle. For them it was much better than coffee. They would climb into one of the abandoned tanker cars, which they had furnished with stools and a small table. In the winter they ran an industrial propane hose through a small hole they'd secretly drilled in the side of the tank. Inside the tank the hose was connected to a large burner that was lit and kept them warm while they became intoxicated with smoke.

One particularly frigid day just before the morning break, Gavin, the youngest, was called to the office across the yard, and his brothers didn't wait for him when the break whistle sounded. He ran back as fast as he could to get his portion of the morning smoke, but when he saw that his brothers were gone, he knew they hadn't waited for him. His face reddened with legendary Scottish anger, knowing they were inside smoking without him.

He hatched a plan to get even. Gavin quietly folded the propane hose that heated the inside of the tanker and giggled quietly as he heard Tavish inside say to Blane, "Hey, the heater went out. We must be out of gas."

Blane said, "Turn up that valve a little, maybe it needs to be opened more."

"Yeah, this joint's out too. Gimme the lighter," Tavish commanded.

About that time, Gavin released his pinch on the gas line outside, and a strong, hissing flow of propane again shot into the tanker. He heard the distinctive clicking of the lighter as his brothers tried to light up their reefer again.

A loud KATOOOF!! belched forth, a blast of flame bursting open the tanker-access hatch on top of the car. Gavin recoiled backwards and stumbled to the ground, crab-crawling a few yards away. He looked up to see big brother Tavish, his red beard and hair billowing smoke, blast wide-eyed from the bowels of the tank.

I once heard an old gal from rural Texas describe a similar scene this way: "Why, he come a tearin' outta thar like a house afire!"

Blane, in a similar shocked state of smoldering, flew furiously out of the hole, and they both chased after Gavin, already up and making his escape. Smoke trailed them past their

stunned coworkers and gate security, and they overtook Gavin in the parking lot trying to start their car. A savage public pummeling alerted a passing patrol car, which radioed for backup. The guns and drugs inside the vehicle and on their persons led to a search warrant for the Scotchmen's home. The MacLean clan is apparently still working together as a prison welding team in the shop at the Texas Department of Corrections. Their house was condemned and demolished.

Perhaps you wonder what in the world this story is doing in a Christian book about missions. My best answer is, in His infinite wisdom, God needed to show me many people, places, and situations I didn't like, in order to steer me toward the mission He wanted for me. It's like a pinball machine: The ball has to be repelled from one area of the table to position it elsewhere. My oil field missions and the world of ships, shipyards, harbors, docks, and warehouses have taken me down many secret passageways on several continents. I got a close look at who and what I didn't want to be. It's enough to drive a man to church.

What about you? Ever see anything that made you turn back toward the Lord?

"Be alert and of sober mind. Your enemy the devil prowls around like a roaring lion looking for someone to devour. Resist him, standing firm in the faith, because you know that the family of believers throughout the world is undergoing the same kind of sufferings."

—1 Peter 5:8-9

Put that in your pipe and smoke it. ❧

26

THE RED CHINESE

"Oh, when them cotton bolls get rotten, you can't pick very much cotton."

—Leadbelly, "Cotton Fields"

I WAS POISONED BY THE CHINESE government, but it's hard for me to blame them when my companions and I were such willing volunteers.

It started in Singapore when I was hired to help train the Chinese in oil and gas exploration. The crew gathered in Hong Kong and flew into the People's Republic of China. We landed in the northern city of Tianjin, about three hours by car from Beijing. The twelve of us were hustled onto a cargo truck with our gear for a ride across town.

At the hotel, we were told to change into the nicest clothes we had for a special dinner. We entered an enormous banquet hall brimming with communist Chinese government officials. They clapped and cheered as if we were rock stars. We were stunned, as none of our team had been informed about this. To us, this was just another oil exploration job site. To our Chinese hosts and our own government, however, it was much more.

Our project represented a new era in Sino-American relations. Seismic exploration was new in China. Our company sold them high-tech equipment called Teleseis, along with all the goodies to go with it. We were the training team for this new technology. It wasn't until we walked into the banquet hall that we all began to realize the magnitude of the moment. In

1985, China was just beginning to "thaw out" a little. President Richard Nixon had visited just thirteen years before. Few Americans traveled there yet.

Our American diplomatic supervisor came to our tables and gave us a pep talk. We had been in the country for approximately two hours. "Be polite and friendly," he counseled. "Their customs are different, which you will see. They are playful and like to sing and tell jokes after dinner. Just go along and do whatever they ask you to do." Then the supervisor left for another appointment. Not a good move. We twelve new crew members, often referred to as "hounds," were left alone in the hall with some seventy-five dignitaries, many of whom were high-ranking military by the looks of all the brass.

Dinner was a dizzying assortment of crab, chicken, lamb, and shellfish, surrounded by every kind of pickled delicacy you can imagine. Tsingtao beer was the only drink offered other than water in big jars on the table. One difference you'd notice at a rather formal state dinner in China is trash disposal. A round lazy Susan is constantly spinning in the center of each table. Initially it is for the distribution of food and condiments like back home. However, as the evening progresses, it is the depository for the unwanted trash from your plate. As the dinner progressed and the beer flowed, we rather enjoyed flinging our crab shells, beer bottles, and chicken bones into the center of the table. By the end of dinner we'd compiled a small mountain of garbage.

It was then that the insidious Chinese plot against us thickened. The toasting began …

It started innocently enough. They placed shot glasses in front of each crew member and toasted our two countries. As per their instructions, we were not to sip the clear liquid, but shoot it back. We did what we were told.

Maotai is a Chinese rice whiskey that goes down about as smooth as battery acid. We all gagged and coughed as they laughed and refilled our glasses. The second shot wasn't as bad as the first, and a steady string of speakers, singers, storytellers, and toasters began to take the stage. There was a song, then we took a shot, then a toast and another shot. The glass-filling cheerleaders kept coming around encouraging us to drink and keep up with the fast-moving military pace and, hey, it was for Sino-American relations. We had to make America look good, didn't we? Well, we didn't.

We fell right into their sinister trap. The Chinese had been to this barbecue before and they, having home field advantage, took to the stage first before the drinking got too deep. Then it was our turn to get up there and show them what we were made of. And we did. Oh, we did.

Have you ever heard the phrase "drunker than Cooter Brown?" Legend has it that Cooter lived on the line between the North and South during the American Civil War and had family on both sides. He didn't want to fight, so he stayed drunk and useless throughout the entire war.

We were in a giant banquet hall in the People's Republic of China. It was our first day. We were being honored at a formal dinner, surrounded by Chinese big shots. We were each now being asked to take the stage and say a few words or sing a song about our homeland. We were hammered.

Some people claim that there's a woman to blame But I know, it's my own damn fault."

—Jimmy Buffett

Our table was filled with Cooter Browns that night. It must have been a pitiful sight, but mercifully, I don't remember a thing. The supervisor thundered at us, in the midst of my excruciating hangover the next morning, that I had sung not one but two songs to the crowd that night. I started with "Dixie," got jazzed when the crowd started clapping, then did it over and over and over: "Well, I wish I was in Dixie, away! away! In Dixieland I'll take my stand to live and die in Dixie. Away, away, away down south in Dixie!"

The people cheered, and the guys said I was a total hit… until I insisted on an encore. The master of ceremonies was trying to pry the microphone from my hand after about the fifth chorus, when I broke into "Them Old Cotton Fields Back Home." A couple of the guys from my crew came up and muscled me unceremoniously off the stage while I was still yowling from the top of my lungs, "Way down in Looziana, just about a mile from Texarkana, in them old cotton fields back home …"

The evening concluded when our English navigator got into a shouting and shoving match with our Australian mechanic. They knocked beer bottles to the floor, it turned to blows, and we were all suddenly dismissed.

This was a bad start for our mission to China. 🐎

It isn't smart to get drunk! Drinking makes a fool of you and leads to fights.

—Proverbs 20:1

27

MOONSTRUCK

"You shall have no other gods before me."

—Exodus 20:3

MY FRIEND MARK BAKER was at the top of our high school class. No one could have guessed that the train wreck of his hopes and dreams lay just around the corner from the grand speeches and parties of our graduation ceremony. Mark convinced me, and I convinced my parents, that it would be worthwhile to attend a summer college prep session at a small college in California. We were roommates in the dormitory and attended the same classes.

Mark burst into our room wild-eyed one afternoon, waving an official-looking letter. "I'm in! I'm in! The University of California at Berkeley! I can't believe it! I have dreamed of this day since I was born! Berkeley, baby, here I come!" It was the happiest day of his life.

Mark borrowed a friend's car for the weekend to look around Berkeley and secure living quarters for the fall semester. His parents called to say how very proud they were for all his years of hard work. I was excited for all of them and sent him off with a handshake and a bear hug.

Sunday came and went with no word from Mark. The guy who loaned Mark the car was very upset. "Where's Mark?!" he pleaded. It was late, but I knew nothing.

Monday by 2:00 p.m., I received a note from the dean asking me to his office. I knew what he wanted, but I had no information about Mark's whereabouts. "Where did he go, Steve?"

"Berkeley." That's all I knew.

Tuesday around lunchtime I got a call from Mark's dad in Los Angeles. He was badly shaken. "It's just not like Mark! He never does stuff like this. Something is wrong, Steve. Think! Did he say anything about where he might be going? He did not attend the orientation at Berkeley. Where did he go?"

I had nothing.

At 10 o'clock Tuesday lights out, the kid who owned the car Mark had borrowed was frantic. "I'm calling the police tomorrow!" I think Mark's dad already had filed a missing person report. Everyone was on edge.

I woke to quiet mumbling and movement in my room around 2:00 a.m. In the dim light of the hallway through the open door, I could see three unfamiliar sets of eyes looking in and watching. Mark was quietly packing a suitcase, sneaking around so as not to wake me. I snapped on the light and got a good look at his startled face. His clothes were smudged and dirty. My first impression was that he had been sleeping on the ground.

"What's going on, Mark? Everyone's been worried. Where've you been?"

He put his finger to his lips to keep me quiet. "Well, I'm sorry if I worried anyone," he began. "Here are the car keys. Please give them back to Scottie."

"He's been out of his mind!" I said. "So has your dad! I think they've both called the police already." As he continued stuffing his suitcase, Mark repeatedly looked toward the quiet strangers who were peeking around the door from the hallway.

"Look, I don't have much time," he said. His tone was hushed and unnatural. "I've met some nice people I want to spend time with. I'm already in at Berkeley, so I don't need this summer session. I'll be in Sacramento the rest of the summer before school starts."

"Sacramento? What's in Sacramento? You mean you're leaving right now?! Wait a minute, man. Who are these people? Have you told your dad any of this?"

He closed his suitcase. "Like I said, I don't have much time." He again glanced at the quiet but visually beckoning figures at the door. "Anything I leave in this room is yours. I don't need it anymore. You're a good friend, Steve." He looked me in the eye and shook my hand.

"Hang on, Mark. What's all this about?"

He handed me a strange card that read "Creative Community Project." "I've met some nice people. Don't worry. I'll call you from Berkeley in September. You can come stay in the apartment I found. It's cool! You'll love it. Now, have a great summer."

"But what about your parents?"

"I'll give my dad a call. He'll be okay. Gotta go." He shook my hand.

I got up and went to the door in time to see two men and a woman touching Mark. They seemed to be physically hustling him down the hall and out the door. Two of them repeatedly looked back, as if someone were going to give chase.

I never saw Mark Baker again.

"A word to the wise ain't necessary—it's the stupid ones that need the advice."

—Bill Cosby

"The Moonies!" our dean of students shrieked when I showed him the card Mark left behind. The Reverend Sun Myung Moon and his Unification Church followers had a long history of brainwashing students. The Moonies were a huge cult, and Mark was being drawn into their midst. I called his parents in LA and told them what I knew. They were devastated.

Summer school ended, and I went home to Texas. Life rolled along.

***

Ten years later, the phone rang. It was an old friend from high school. She invited me to a high school class reunion and asked if I would be willing to help track down old classmates. I received an email with several names and last known contact information. Mark's name hit me like a brick. I called the same house in LA where I'd stayed with Mark years before, and his father answered.

There was a long silence before the interrogation began. Dr. Baker clearly did not trust me.

"What school did you say you went to with my son? What year? Who was the headmaster there? What's your middle name? What are your parents' names? I'm looking at your yearbook. Did you have short hair or long?"

He finally believed who I was and spilled the whole horrible tale. The Moonies took Mark hook, line and sinker. Swallowed him whole. He was completely indoctrinated and committed into the cult. He worshipped and served Reverend Sun Myung Moon and his Unification Church with everything he had, physically, emotionally and financially. In the first year, he spoke to his family very briefly only twice. He didn't speak to them at all during the following three years.

By year five, when the Moonies started trying to access Mark's inherited family assets, the family had had just about enough. They hired a professional kidnapper to get Mark out. Mark was apprehended in California, bound, gagged, blindfolded, tossed in a trunk, and driven to a secret location across the country in North Carolina for "deprogramming."

This process took months, and Mark screamed a lot in his padded cell. It probably wasn't even legal, but his father didn't care. Mark was bitter but eventually saw the light. A huge portion of his life had been stolen from him. His recovery counselors advised him and his father that, though  his recovery was complete, as a precaution, Mark should never have any contact with cult members and never return to the state of California. He apparently never has, and he never attended the University of California at Berkeley.

Many things today, many seemingly harmless things, will draw your attention far away from the Lord and the mission He has crafted for you. Beware of those who would attract you to something other than Christ.

Have you ever been tempted to try something like this? ❧

But there were also false prophets among the people, just as there will be false teachers among you. They will secretly introduce destructive heresies, even denying the sovereign Lord who bought them—bringing swift destruction on themselves.

—2 Peter 2:1

28

IWA

"And once the storm is over you won't remember how you made it through, how you managed to survive. You won't even be sure, in fact, whether the storm is really over. But one thing is certain. When you come out of the storm you won't be the same person who walked in."

—Haruki Murakami

HAS GOD EVER LED YOU through devastation to show you your mission? I woke up one day thinking I knew where life was going. I thought I knew my mission that day. I thought I was in control. The next day, God revealed a new clue to the mission He was designing for me. It got my attention.

The sun was bright, and gentle trade winds kept the Hawaiian Islands cool and tranquil. I worked for Kauai Building and Supply delivering sheetrock and other materials to construction sites around the island. It was a beautiful island.

The public warning came just three hours before Hurricane Iwa hit us like an atomic bomb. The storm had suddenly changed course in the Pacific and was now racing straight toward us. My friend, Marley, and I fled to the condo, but policemen said we were too close to the water and could not stay in our own home, nor could we go to our warehouse in Kapaa. We simply could not stay near the shore.

"But where are we supposed to go?" we pleaded with the officers.

"Away from the coast," came the unsympathetic reply.

We drove up-country to the home of Paul Priggie, a warehouse employee. He and his wife, Mary, were barricading their flimsy house. We helped them get ready, ate a somber dinner, then waited and prayed.

The storm unloaded on us like an artillery barrage, and we scrambled like mice under the beds. Mary prayed out loud continuously, and with each monstrous gust torrentially raining debris on our roof she hollered, "Dear Jesus! Mother Mary! God, please save us!"

The house shook, and I thought of Dorothy and Toto flying to Munchkin Land in the cyclone. Death or dismemberment seemed likely to strike us at any moment, with whole trees snapping off and blowing past our shanty. After a couple of hours, we saw the eerie calm in the eye of the storm, then the second half of the hurricane slammed in again, pummeling us without mercy.

We opened the door the next morning and couldn't believe our eyes. Iwa had had the effect of a nuclear blast. We climbed out the window and used a chainsaw to clear trees and open the front door of the house. The mass destruction indicated that bodies must be a certainty, but there weren't any. No one died that we knew of, but what a deathly looking mess. The place was trashed, boats sunk, buildings destroyed, homes and property gone with the wind. What had been a bright and happy place the day before looked like a war zone.

There was a spirit of sadness, thankfulness, hope, and brotherly love. People prayed and spoke of the Lord openly that day, I do assure you. A US submarine pulled into Nawiliwili Harbor and gave us power. I ran the barbecue and served food at the Red Cross refuge in an elementary school full of cots. We dressed minor injuries, hugged a lot of people, and helped

pick up the pieces on Thanksgiving Day 1982. It was my first disaster.

Has disaster, natural or man-made, ever changed the way you look at the world? ❧

"And that same day the Lord sent thunder and rain. So all the people stood in awe of the Lord."

—1 Samuel 12:18

29

THE BUSINESS END

"I have been doomed to such a dreadful shipwreck: that man is not truly one, but truly two."

The Strange Case of Dr. Jekyll and Mr. Hyde
Robert Louis Stevenson

I USED TO WORK WITH an Irish carpenter on the island of Roatán in the Bay Islands of Honduras. Sean Galloway fashioned the most beautiful hardwood staircases, floors, and cabinetry. He played the guitar and sang heartfelt Irish tunes. He could be thoughtful and quite a gentleman.

Sean was also what I would characterize as a "Jekyll-and-Hyde" drunk. By day, he dressed the interiors of new homes with dedicated, magical craftsmanship. His clients loved him, but after five o'clock he began to drink beer, and rum always followed. Every single night, Sean Galloway transformed himself into someone no one wanted to be around.

Sean took on a look and tone that signaled the metamorphosis. Everyone who knew him understood when it was time to keep a safe distance. The danger signs became more evident with each passing drink. It started with rudeness and quickly escalated into harassing women, exchanging angry words with a tourist, or even starting a full-scale barroom brawl. I witnessed this with my own eyes on more than one occasion, just like in the movies.

I busted a chair right across his teeth
And we crashed through the wall and into the street
Kicking and a' gouging in the mud and the blood and the beer.

—Johnny Cash, "A Boy Named Sue"

The next morning, though he might be sporting cuts and bruises from a brawl the night before, mild-mannered Dr. Jekyll returned. Always cheerful, Sean sipped coffee and whistled while he worked. He usually did not remember much of anything that had happened. I've seen plenty of drunks in my time, but never anyone like him.

Sean was a Vietnam veteran. He told me stories about the ride to Khe Sanh and how they'd sit on their helmets to protect themselves from the ground fire that came up through the floor of the helicopter. Khe Sanh was a notorious place, known for extensive violence and death during the 1968 Tet Offensive. Sean killed people and saw friends die. He had been wounded multiple times. Maybe that explains why he drank so much.

One afternoon I had to get some tools from Sean's house. It was a Saturday, so he was not at work. The minute he spoke, I knew he had been drinking heavily. It was abnormal for him to drink during the day, as he usually observed the "five o'clock rule." But on this day, for whatever reason, five o'clock had clearly arrived early.

Sean began insisting I have a drink with him, and I knew I was in trouble. As diplomatically as possible, I explained I had work to do, and though I would like to, I couldn't stay. I backed cautiously, little by little, toward the door.

Sean picked up a nickel-plated .44 Magnum revolver off the counter and pointed it at me.

I took another careful step. "I really gotta go, Sean." I could clearly see the Black Talon rounds rotate in the cylinder when he cocked the hammer with his thumb. "Halt!" He garbled a command. I looked straight down the barrel, and I knew all too well what would come out if it discharged.

I knew this man and his current mental state. I knew this  gun and the destructive power of the bullets in it. I also knew the immortal words from the movie Dirty Harry: "But being as this is a .44 Magnum, the most powerful handgun in the world, and would blow your head clean off, you've got to ask yourself one question: Do I feel lucky?"

I didn't feel lucky at all looking down the business end of that weapon, but I knew I couldn't stay there. So I quietly raised my hands just like in the old western movies when the outlaw has the drop on you, and I remember softly humming as I backed to the door, carefully opened it, and walked out. The gun was trained on me the whole time as Sean Galloway grumbled and snarled through his oversized mustache like Yosemite Sam. I didn't stop shaking for over an hour, but I was glad to be out of there.

"And I'm tellin' ya son, well it ain't no fun starin' straight down a .44."

—Lynrd Skynrd, "Gimme Three Steps"

My relationship with Sean and with the Lord changed that day. One ended, the other became more valuable. Sean didn't remember a thing the next morning as he whistled and drank

his coffee, but I did. Sometimes no matter how much you may like someone and pray for them, you gotta sever your ties and cut 'em loose.

Have you ever had to toss someone on the scrap heap and end the relationship? Maybe it was someone from high school you really cared about, but they just weren't good for your life. It may not be easy, but sometimes it's best. ❧

Walk with the wise and become wise, for a companion of fools suffers harm.

—Proverbs 13:20

30

AN OLD TRADE

"When Israel was in Egypt land: Let my people go.
Oppress'd so hard they could not stand: Let my people go.
Go down, Moses, way down in Egypt land,
Tell old Pharaoh: Let my people go."

— "Go Down Moses" - Jubilee Singers 1872
Slave Songs of the Underground Railroad

I USED TO THINK SLAVERY was ancient history, like back in Civil War days. I learned about slavery in movies about cotton plantations and folks from Africa years ago. The way I mostly heard it, early on at least, slaves were lucky to have masters who loved them and treated them like family. It was a romanticized view of farms full of slaves who did whatever the handsome, well-dressed owners wanted. I remember Mammy, Prissy, and all the rest in the famous movie *Gone with the Wind*:

There was a land of cavaliers and cotton fields called the Old South.... Here in this pretty world gallantry took its last bow.... Here was the last ever to be seen of knights and their ladies fair, of master and of slave.... Look for it only in books, for it is no more than a dream remembered. A civilization gone with the wind.

As time went by, films like *Amistad* and *Amazing Grace* brought us a clearer picture of the horrific reality of the slave trade, and that's the way I came to view it. Slavery was an "old trade," something that really was gone with the wind, as far as I could tell in my homogenized little Texas world. People didn't buy and sell human beings anymore. Did they? I could see racial injustice and discrimination, to be sure. However, I could see no trace of real slavery. I was certain it was a thing of the past. That is, until I began to travel. ❧

31

BOXES OF BULLETS

I WAS INVITED ON A GENUINE big-game hunting safari in Africa. It was the real deal. Our tented camp was located in the Kizigo Game Reserve of central Tanzania, just north of the Nijombi River and Ruaha National Park, out in the middle of nowhere. Some may not like the idea of hunting, but being born and raised a hunter from Texas, I was in heaven. I was Teddy Roosevelt on safari. I was Robert Redford in *Out of Africa*. It was the stuff of dreams.

"You know you are truly alive when you are living among lions."

—Isak Dinesen

We were attended by two white hunting guides and thirty local men, referred to as "bwana boys," who cooked, cleaned, served, kept order around camp, drove vehicles, and functioned as animal trackers and skinners. John was my personal gun bearer. He quickly established the nature of our relationship on the first long day of hunting. I was tired and dozing in the back of the Land Rover when the vehicle ground to an abrupt halt.

John grabbed a .375 H&H Magnum bolt-action rifle from the gun rack, cycled a cartridge into the chamber, hoisted me physically by the arm to a standing position, and thrust the weapon at me. He clenched my shoulder with one powerful hand for stability, and with the other he pointed about two hundred yards away to a grazing antelope, locally called a greater kudu. He commanded me with seasoned authority, "Shoot, Bwana!"

As if by John's will, I dropped the thing dead like a sack of potatoes. John's intense eyes immediately turned joyful, and a grin spread across his jet-black face as he vigorously pumped my hand with a hardy "Well done, old boy! Well done!" We became fast friends.

John also served as an agent for the Tanzanian government to "verify the kill" on safari. Hefty government permit fees are charged to hunters for the killing of each animal. If an animal is wounded but gets away, you don't get another chance; you bought it. The rationale is that a wounded animal is a dead animal, whether you locate it or not. John was the official who made the call whether an animal had been wounded.

Some weeks later, I took a long shot at an impala with my Weatherby .270. I was sure I missed cleanly, but as with every shot you attempt, trackers were released to be certain. We checked the intended location of the "hit" and found no trace of blood. The area was searched carefully, but just as we were about to return to the truck, John called our attention to a single spot of blood on the ground. It was about the size of a single discharge from the average eyedropper, and John was the only one standing around the area when we were all searching. It always made me wonder.

John marked it as a "kill" on his sheet and expressed his apologies over my protests. That was that; I had to pay the permit fee.

John called me away from the campfire that evening. He explained he didn't normally do this kind of thing, but if I would be willing to give him forty US dollars and two boxes of the .375 Magnum shells, he would be willing to look the other way, scratch the kill off his sheet, and allow me another shot at an impala the next morning. I readily agreed and was happy to have made the deal.

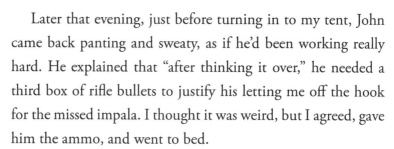

Later that evening, just before turning in to my tent, John came back panting and sweaty, as if he'd been working really hard. He explained that "after thinking it over," he needed a third box of rifle bullets to justify his letting me off the hook for the missed impala. I thought it was weird, but I agreed, gave him the ammo, and went to bed.

A couple of days later on the drive back to the airstrip and our flights to Arusha, I asked our guide Armando about John's strange behavior that night. Armando laughed and said, "Oh, he was really happy with the person you helped him purchase."

I stared blankly.

"John made an arrangement with the chief of a nearby village," Armando explained. "Two boxes of bullets and forty dollars could buy John an eighteen-year-old girl from among the tribal families. John ran over there that night with payment, and the chief informed him that with one more box of shells, he could select a 'wife' from among the fourteen-year-old girls. That's why he ran back for more."

I was sickened and didn't want to believe it, but it was true. John the gun bearer had used my money and ammunition to purchase another human being outright. He had made payment, collected the merchandise, and took the girl to work at his home hundreds of miles away. I met this young girl, and she was real live chattel.

"You leave that gal alone. She's mine! Bought and paid for."

—Lonesome Dove

She would live in the company of a stranger who bought her like an animal, and she would likely never see the Nijombi River, her village, or her family in the Kizigo Game Reserve again.

We use the term loosely in our society, but have you ever seen true oppression? Dictionary.com defines it as "the exercise of authority or power in a burdensome, cruel, or unjust manner." Slavery is about as oppressed as one can be, and it exists worldwide. The Bible speaks about oppression repeatedly, and fighting it is central to our mission.

Have you ever seen oppression for real? ❦

"Whoever oppresses the poor shows contempt for their Maker, but whoever is kind to the needy honors God."

—Proverbs 14:31

32

PATPONG

"Bangkok, like Las Vegas, sounds like a place where you make bad decisions."

—Todd Phillips, producer of *The Hangover*

T HERE ARE CERTAIN PARTS of my life I have not wanted my wife and young daughters to know about. The following is certainly one of those parts. However, in sharing with others about my life and how God shaped my heart toward missionary service, I would be terribly remiss in excluding darker parts just to save face. These were key components in the Lord's Master Plan to gain my attention and steer my course.

I ask myself whether it's worth it to share this risky information. But if I get the attention of some guy out there who mistakenly thinks the Lord has no use for him because he has been in unclean places and led a life Jesus would not approve of, my answer has to be yes, it is worth it. If someday I get to meet that guy in heaven because of something he read here, or if just one person gets actively involved in missions and saves some of these kids from a life of slavery, then yes, it's worth it.

One day I woke up to the realization that it was the Lord who led me to some of the world's more unsavory places. He had something to show and teach me there. Wherever it is you've been and whatever it is you've been doing, you must understand that it is He, God Himself, who put you in that set of circumstances to teach you something. The question is: Are you learning, and are you willing to use your experience to serve Him now?

So, in the hope of turning one other person, perhaps some piece of oil field trash, toward the Lord's service, here is my story.

I arrived by myself in Thailand in 1985. I was twenty-four years old, and I thought I had died and gone to heaven. People often ask which is my favorite country, and Thailand pops into my mind. It has wonderful food, geography, handicrafts, a rich history, architecture, and some of the nicest and most creative people in the world.

I toured the country, visiting beaches, temples, and bull-fights. I trekked into the hill country by the Burma and Laotian border. I spent most of my initial time there in the northern town of Chiang Mai. It was a small town back then.

The girls in Thailand are beautiful, and I was a young, single American with a clean shirt and new tennis shoes. Back home in Texas I was nobody special, but in Southeast Asia, I might as well have been a movie star or famous sports figure. I felt like one of the Beatles with girls chasing me down the street. Everywhere I went, beautiful girls smiled, waved, and came over to talk with me. I would be sitting in a public place, minding my own business, and girls in their late teens and early twenties would start talking to me, competing with each other for my attention.

"Well, we're big rock singers. We got golden fingers.
And we're loved everywhere we go.

—Dr. Hook and the Medicine Show, "The Cover of the Rolling Stone"

I went out on dates with several beautiful girls in Thailand. It was as big an ego trip as I've ever been on. I was somebody. They loved me because, quite obviously to me, I was great.

So where was God in all this? First, having me observe and admire these beautiful people allowed me to talk with them and get to know them, growing a deep love for their customs and way of life. Dating girls allowed me to develop a special connection with Thai people. (I even considered marriage more than once, but was afraid of what my mother might say.)

Second, God showed me their dilemma of poverty and just how privileged I had been. In getting to know these girls, I also got to know a little about who they were, where they came from, what their parents did, what they had, and what they didn't have. Their choices in life were very limited. I began to better understand their attraction to me, or to any foreigner who could offer the opportunity to get out of their world and into another one. They didn't see me as exceptionally attractive. They saw me as a chance to win the lottery and take off for America. Turns out I wasn't a rock star after all.

Third, God showed me the brutal, organized, and sinister way these beautiful, gentle young girls are captured, enslaved, systematically humiliated, and sold like animals. He led me to love these people and this culture, and then God stabbed me in the gut and left me with a deep, agonizing pain I still feel today.

Have you ever asked, "Why, God?" Well, I have, and why God chose to show me like this I don't know, but I will never forget it.

I was hired by a Singapore-based oil exploration company in China staffed mostly with Vietnam veterans from the US military. I was never in the military, but I felt like I was sometimes. Our operation in China was run with military efficiency. These guys knew the ropes in Asia and often referred to Asian

people as "gooks," "slopes," or "zipper heads." Many of our team members had either been wounded by Asians or had friends wounded or killed in the war.

Thailand was the most popular rest and recuperation (R & R) spot during the war in Southeast Asia. I told my oil field buddies I already knew my way around Thailand, and they laughed. "You don't know Thailand like we do!" they roared. "Come with us, greenhorn. We'll show you around." They took me to Bangkok.

We arrived at the Patpong District as the Asian sun was setting on the big city. Located on the long streets called Silom Road and Surawong Road, Patpong is still one of the biggest red-light districts in the entire world. This is where my military coworkers took me for my "education." I have since seen movies about Vietnam with scenes of brothels and loud bars with naked girls dancing and propositioning men all over the place. Believe me when I tell you that nothing I have seen in the movies can come close to conveying the dizzying assault on one's senses I saw in real life when I was twenty-four years old in Bangkok. It is beyond my ability to describe.

"Man, I spent six years living right on top of the raunchiest whorehouse in the PI."

—Richard Gere - An Officer and a Gentleman

We went into several bars for beer, and in each one partially naked girls threw themselves at us, always with a passionate invitation to go upstairs. The price was "cheap-cheap." In some of these places there were the most disgusting and degrading floorshows imaginable. In the streets, male as well as female prostitutes were absolutely everywhere, calling to us to come on over. Most Americans, indeed most people on earth, certainly proper people, can't possibly imagine this environment, as there is nothing to compare it to where they live. You can't believe this is just "normal life" for thousands of these young men and women. A couple of the guys I was with did pay and go upstairs, but I didn't. It made me sad and disgusted. I thought of the Thai girls I knew in Chiang Mai.

Looking back, I see God's fingerprints all over this experience.

My military buddies explained to me how pimps, or "employment agents," scour the countryside of rural Thailand, Cambodia, Laos, and Burma looking for poor families who can't care for their kids. They offer payment for young girls to come work in Bangkok as secretaries or restaurant staff. The legal guardianship of the children is signed over to these agents by their impoverished parents, and girls are forced into indentured service. They are enslaved to the business for a period of years until they are "paid off" to the house. They are bought-and-sold slaves, some of them before they reach their tenth birthday.

Today I think of my daughters and how they might feel if I sold them to some stranger for money and they never saw me or their mother again. It is hard for us in the West to really comprehend, but the sale of young people happens all the time in poor countries around the world. The girls dancing in those bars are trying to make enough money to buy their freedom from bondage, but in the process they are degraded as badly as any human beings on earth.

Did you ever see anything like this? Thousands of innocent children are being consumed every year by an obscene marketplace with an insatiable appetite, especially in the third world. The exponential spread of pornography on the Internet has created all kinds of new markets for oppressed, degraded, and enslaved young people. Our mission is to provide a few of these kids with safety, protection, a future, and a sound relationship with Jesus Christ.

Do you want to help? ❧

Children are a heritage from the Lord, offspring a reward from Him.

—Psalm 127:3

33

THE FISHBOWL

"They swim around, all day in a pool, And never have to go to school."

— *Theodore Cleaver in Leave It to Beaver*

THE FISHBOWL WAS AN ELEGANT PLACE we went for dinner on Phuket Island. I knew there would be girls, but it wasn't the average establishment. Inside were Arabs wearing robes and turbans, guys from Africa, numerous Westerners, some military, and a few Thai men. A nicely dressed waitress escorted us to our table, gave us menus, and took our drink orders. There were many girls serving the tables and talking to the men. This was normal for Thailand.

Two large, round windows located at the far end of the restaurant were closed by long, flowing curtains. A tuxedo-clad announcer greeted the crowd warmly and prepared us for the main attraction during dinner. He pulled back the curtains on the enormous, bulging fish-eye windows and revealed perhaps two hundred young girls wandering around behind them.

They were mostly between junior high and high school age. Each was well dressed, with a numbered card pinned to her lapel. True to the name, it did indeed resemble two large fishbowls with a bunch of "fish" all swimming around inside. I was absolutely stunned as the crowd clapped and whistled wildly.

The bidding started when the announcer began calling out numbers and girls obediently stepped forward to be viewed. We were in a high-priced auction house, and the excited men started screaming their bids. The younger the girl, the higher the price. Virgins commanded a premium price. They were orphaned and abandoned children who'd been captured, cleaned, brushed like show horses, and sold to the highest bidder. This happened to these children every night!

I witnessed ugly old Arab men picking numbers out of the fishbowl and disappearing upstairs with young girls who should have been at home with families who loved them, going to school. I felt a deep sadness when I saw their helpless eyes. I saw them as human, not fish for sale to be consumed.

It was the most unfair and inhuman thing I have ever witnessed, and I was marked for life.

"Learn to do right; seek justice. Defend the oppressed. Take up the cause of the fatherless; plead the case of the widow."
—Isaiah 1:17

Years later I was in New Orleans with some of my cousins, and for fun they wanted to go in some strip club off Bourbon Street. They thought it was weird I didn't want to go in with them for a giggle, but I didn't care. I remembered the look in the eyes of those young girls I saw being led away by strangers in Thailand.

There is a scene in the James Bond movie, *Never Say Never Again*, where the beautiful blond actress, Kim Basinger, is tied to a slave trading post, partially undressed and presented for sale to a bunch of ugly, lecherous Bedouin buyers. I think of Thailand every time I see it.

Sheri and I went out on one of our date nights for dinner and a movie. When we saw the movie *Amazing Grace*, the story of William Wilberforce's fight against African slavery in England, I cried like a baby at the ending when slavery was abolished. However, my tears were not so much for Africans in the 1700s as for innocent Asian slaves.

My loved ones may not know it, at least not until now, but our missionary work with orphanages, Christian education, and giving kids in impoverished communities a chance at life is, in part, a direct result of the slavery I have seen passing through the tourist areas and bars of Thailand, Singapore, Indonesia, Cuba, Ecuador, Hong Kong, Kenya, Mexico, Guatemala, Amsterdam, Oman, Germany, France, Prague, New Orleans, and elsewhere around the world. Without seeing it for myself, I would not have been aware of the enormity of this problem and most likely would not have cared.

Do not ever underestimate the things God is showing you, weaving into your life and into your heart for the mission of building His Kingdom. Dig deep, and consult with Him every day. You have more to offer than you may think. ❧

"And we know that in all things God works for the good of those who love him, who have been called according to his purpose."

—Romans 8:28

34

THE ERRAND

"You are not here merely to make a living. You are here in order to enable the world to live more amply, with greater vision, with a finer spirit of hope and achievement. You are here to enrich the world, and you impoverish yourself if you forget the errand."

—Woodrow Wilson

M Y JACQUES COUSTEAU DREAMS came true in the Galapagos Islands. Shortly after being licensed as a scuba diving instructor, I landed a job as an underwater wildlife guide, closed my house in Austin, sold my car, and moved to South America. If you ever want to run away from it all, Ecuador is good a hideout. A little more about that later.

It was an amazing time. Then, just like that, my tour of duty was over. I wanted to stay in Ecuador, but the only thing I could find in the way of employment was an occasional day as a substitute teacher at the American School of Quito. Babysitting spoiled, rich Ecuadorean children quickly took its toll, and in a few weeks I was on the last rung of the ladder. I had lunch one day with a fellow Galapagos guide, Albert, who owned a travel agency in Quito. He suggested that before I retreated to the States, if I wasn't in too much a hurry, I might consider "running an errand" for him. I couldn't believe what he told me next.

Albert built his travel business through friendships with local Ecuadoreans. One of these unique relationships was with the Waodoni, a tribe of real live Amazon jungle Indians historically known as the Aucas. The tribe had reached an agreement with Albert that it would be mutually beneficial for them to construct a small tourist "lodge" in their remote village to host tourists and make needed money. Albert could not take two or three weeks off work to go down there and motivate them to get started, so he wanted me to go as his ambassador. Floored to the toenails, I accepted without many questions. The idea of high adventure and valued service to others attracted me. It was an exotic mission.

I arrived at the rendezvous point in Shell Mera, a remote outpost some ten hours down a bumpy road from Quito on the edge of the Amazon rain forest. My amiable American guide and pilot, Steve, was busy loading a small plane when I arrived, so I threw my duffle bag on the backseat.

We catapulted eastward off the end of an aging runway and left all civilization behind. The plane soared over a seemingly endless canopy, and I could scarcely contain my excitement. I was glad Steve was going to be with me, because the idea of being with primitive Indians in the middle of the Amazon was a little spooky.

Over the headset microphone in the noisy plane, I asked Steve, "How did a nice guy like you wind up in a place like this?" I figured he was an out-of-work oil field hand.

"My parents moved our family to Ecuador when I was a little boy," he explained. "Dad was a missionary pilot. He and his four friends were involved in a mission project to contact the Waodoni people and bring the Word of God into their lives." The plane buzzed into the late afternoon with the equatorial sun at our backs. I noticed not even a clearing, much less a town or village, just treetops as far as the eye could see on this crystal clear day. We were heading into the middle of nowhere.

"So, you have actually lived down here since you were young?" I probed.

"No," he replied. "We moved back when I was in elementary school, and I finished high school and college up in the States. I got married, had a family, and started my own business."

I was curious. "So your dad's work down here was finished then?"

Steve cracked a broad smile. "Yep! I guess you might put it that way! Their work was definitely finished all right." He laughed openly. "My dad's name was Nate. He and his best friend, Jim, and their fellow missionaries established contact with some of the people you are about to meet. You see, back in the fifties the indigenous people here had never even seen white folks. Dad and his group started making friendships with them by dropping gifts from a plane like this one, and later they actually landed and visited with them."

"So," I said with amazement, "your dad was one of the first people to teach them the Bible?"

"Well, not exactly." Steve hesitated. "Dad and his friends were trying to communicate with them one afternoon when the Waodoni got scared, I guess. For whatever reason, they suddenly felt like these white people were a threat, so they picked up their spears and killed all of them."

"They killed your dad?! You mean the people we're about to visit right now? These people killed your dad?" I gasped in shock.

"Yep. You're about to meet some of them. They speared Dad and his friends to death right there by the side of the river. Then they ripped apart the plane. I guess they must have thought it was an evil spirit or something. The Ecuadorean army found all of their bodies about a week later. Along with Dad there was Jim Elliot, Ed McCully, Pete Fleming, and Roger Youderian."

I soaked in this horrifying news as I peered out the windshield. Over the plane's headset, I had just heard a famous missionary story for the first time from the son of the guy it happened to, on my way to meet the people who did it, in the very place it happened. I was as freaked out as I could be in the heavy silence that followed. The journey had taken on an entirely new and dangerous dimension. My mother wouldn't like me doing this.

"Oh, don't worry," Steve said as if reading my mind. "They're much better now." This was minimal comfort to me.

"Okay, this is it, we're goin' in." I felt the plane begin its descent, but saw nothing but trees.

"In? In where?" I asked as I scanned the immediate direction of our approach. There was nothing but tall forest canopy. I could literally see birds in the treetops before I saw the small clearing. He did a quick dive-bomb maneuver over the grass strip, and then I could see dozens of scantily clad villagers running in our direction.

By the time we touched down and he switched off the engine, we were completely surrounded. The natives were all chattering in the weirdest language I had ever heard as Steve unloaded the plane. I held my duffle bag close to my chest, smiled sheepishly, and was astounded to hear this gringo begin to converse with the Waodoni in their own bizarre tongue. I was in a state of shock.

Steve suddenly spun on his heel, stared for a moment at the setting sun, and glanced at his watch. "Well," extending his hand as he reached to me for a good-bye shake, "I guess this is it for now. Gotta run. I'll see ya in about three weeks."

In utter disbelief, I said nothing, my jaw hanging open, as he walked around to the cockpit door. I stared for a second at the jabbering, savage hoard, some of whom were actually carrying spears and blowguns. I dropped my bag and ran around the plane.

"Wha-wha-what? You're leaving?! I thought you were staying here with me!"

"No." He smiled. "I gotta get home for dinner. Didn't Albert tell you? It's too dangerous to fly out here after sundown. My wife and I have a clinic about three days' walk from here in another part of the jungle. Don't worry. You'll be okay. There's a couple of guys who speak some Spanish. Now please close the door and step back."

The engine roared to life as Steve Saint gunned it down the runway. He barely cleared the treetops at the western end of the strip and disappeared straight into the heart of a brilliant sunset. The darkest night fell quickly after that, and I felt as alone as I had ever been.

I had just met my first Christian missionary.

Who would live in a place like this? ❧

"I couldn't do that. Could you do that? How can they do that? Who are those guys?"

—Butch Cassidy and the Sundance Kid

"People who do not know the Lord ask why in the world we waste our lives as missionaries. They forget they too are expending their lives and when the bubble has burst, they will have nothing of eternal significance to show for the years they have wasted."

—Nate Saint

35

JUNGLE DAN

"I have one desire now—to live a life of reckless abandon for the Lord, putting all my energy and strength into it."

—Ed McCully

I NEVER TOLD MY FAMILY or friends outside of church about my friend Danny, whose missionary parents took him to the Amazon jungle to live with Indians when he was four. They lived down there for fifteen years. Maybe I kept this friendship locked in the "secret passages" of my life because, well, it's an association I had with what I call "extreme faith." It's just the kind of complete and total dedication to the Lord and missions that scares many people. I'm embarrassed to say he scared me at first. Danny's testimony is perhaps the most outlandish real-life journey of anyone I have ever personally known, and he's among the nicest guys you'd ever want to meet.

When Jim Elliot, Nate Saint, Pete Fleming, Ed McCully, and Roger Youderian were speared to death by the Auca Indians in 1956, it made headlines around the world. People were riveted by these "radical" missionaries who had risked everything to bring the gospel of Jesus Christ to unreached people in the Amazon. Jim's widow, Elisabeth Elliot, wrote a book called *Through Gates of Splendor*, and more recently the motion picture *The End of the Spear* told the story from young Steve Saint's perspective.

No missionary story has moved so many people. People like my friend Dan Schoen's father.

Danny was a baby when his dad, working as a carpenter, read the news of the five missionaries killed in Ecuador. Right then and there the Lord told Mr. Schoen to leave his job, become a missionary, gather his family, and move them to the Amazon jungle in South America. I can only imagine his wife's reaction when he burst through the door and told her the news that evening. She evidently felt the calling too and was elated.

I have heard this story directly from Danny only once. Some of it is a bit unclear, but this is what I remember.

It took the Schoen family five years to prepare for their journey. How they decided to serve the Lord in a remote part of the jungle of Suriname, which is next to Brazil, I do not know. This was their calling, and this family with three small children simply took the gospel to people who were feared by the outside world. Most white people who had previously set out for this very inaccessible region of the country had never returned and were never heard from again.

Undeterred, Mr. Schoen and five other missionary families made an agreement with the government of Suriname. If they were allowed to take their young families to live deep in the jungle, they would clear and develop airstrips to access that part of the country. They would also learn the local language, reduce it to writing, teach locals to read and write, provide medical care, preach the gospel, and translate the Bible. The government thought they were crazy, but this offer was attractive and they gave the green light for the group to proceed.

In 1961, the Schoen family packed up their young children and belongings and flew to Paramaribo, the capital of Suriname. There they loaded their family and gear into several primitive canoes and paddled upriver for many days, deep into the uncharted wilderness. They were called to settle and live permanently at an unknown destination in the bush, crawling with wild animals, stinging bugs, and deadly reptiles. It was also certain to be filled with hostile, savage neighbors.

You've gotta love people like this.

They pressed on, praying continuously, until they arrived at the remote location of their land grant in the tribal area. They went ashore, unpacked their gear, cleared the shoreline, and made camp. There they lived for roughly fifteen years. Mr. Schoen began clearing land for a runway. Mrs. Schoen made the best home she could. The kids played and did their chores and schoolwork. The family occasionally saw people watching them from the surrounding jungle, but they would quickly disappear whenever Mr. Schoen approached to say hello.

The first major contact occurred shortly after their arrival in the jungle when Danny was around six years old. A large, powerful native man brought a sick woman in a canoe. He never spoke a word, but the Schoen family recognized she was gravely ill. They cared for her with medicines and prayed almost continuously while the man stood guard. Three days later, the woman's fever broke, she got better, and the couple left quietly.

Some months later, young Danny was playing beside the river and looked up to see perhaps two hundred Indians in canoes, all paddling straight for their camp. He ran screaming to his mother in fear they were under attack and in mortal danger. Much to the Schoens' surprise, however, the tribe quietly came ashore and began building a village all around their camp. One day they were a lone outpost in the jungle, the next day they were in the center of "town." Initially, they didn't understand what had happened, and being the center of tribal attention took a little getting used to.

Time passed, and a relationship began to develop with their new neighbors. Dan's father was a quick study in linguistics, and after a few months of practicing the native language he learned several alarming things.

The first revelation was that a tribal council had been convened when the Schoens arrived in the jungle. There was a strong motion to deal with the family in the traditional manner: Kill them all without delay! The Indians believed previous white people exploring the area were clearly "white spirits" who had come to steal the native children, so they had been speared on the spot. The Schoen family, however, were accompanied by small children. This confused the locals, so rather than kill the Schoens on the spot as was customary, a wait-and-see policy was adopted by the tribe.

The next thing Mr. Schoen learned was that the man who arrived with the sick woman months before was the local shaman, or medicine man. His wife had become ill and he was unable to make her well. So he announced he would take her to the Schoen family camp. If against all odds his wife recovered and lived, the shaman declared he would throw away his charms and trust their white spirit, Jesus. Then the tribe would know Jesus is the "strong one."

The Schoen family lived with the tribe and daily shared Jesus and the Holy Spirit with their new extended family in Suriname. It wasn't long before Danny and his older brother were learning the ways of the jungle, practicing local survival methods and customs, and going with the tribesmen on long hunting trips without their parents.

The result of this bold move by the Schoen family in obedience to the Lord's calling, their willingness to risk everything to share Christ in Suriname, is that over the last fifty-plus years many churches and ministries have developed in that part of the world. Thousands of people have accepted Christ, and all manner of social services have been provided to serve the physical needs of the people. All because of one brave family.

Danny returned to the United States when he was nineteen years old, went to college, and raised a family. Like Steve Saint, he has now returned to the jungle where he grew up. He serves the tribe and continues to grow the ministry. Danny shoots a bow and arrow like nobody's business.

I have since met other missionaries who serve in a variety of ways. They always inspire me. Steve and Danny have left a deep and unforgettable impression.

Have you ever met and visited with a missionary? You might be surprised by what they tell you. ❧

"He is no fool who gives up what he cannot keep to gain what he cannot lose."

—Jim Elliot

36

A SIMPLETON

"Life is hard. It's even harder when you're stupid."

—*John Wayne*

𝕴 HAVE SEEN LOTS OF POOR CHOICES, and in my ignorance, I have made more mistakes than I care to admit. I'm a simple, ordinary guy.

I didn't like the consequences that complicated my happy life or made me feel afraid and stupid. However, pain has raised my awareness and helped steer me toward the Lord, His missions, and a happier existence all around.

Pain is a good navigational tool.

Have the consequences of your thoughts or actions ever led you to have a little talk with God?

The trick is to try and make good choices by following Him who made us, rather than jump to lesser decisions. It is easier said than done. I'm afraid I know.

Life is indeed hard, my friend. But God is good. Stick by God. Bet your life on Him.

If I forget and start to make life complicated, I just remind myself: Keep it simple, stupid. ❦

"Enter through the narrow gate. For wide is the gate and broad is the road that leads to destruction, and many enter through it."

—*Matthew 7:13*

PASSAGE III

MISSIONS: WHY BOTHER?

Stevie Takes a Stab at the Meaning of It All

"Get busy living, or get busy dying."

—Andy Dufresne, The Shawshank Redemption

37

CAST ADRIFT

Wizard: Well, you force me into a cataclysmic decision. The only way to get Dorothy back to Kansas is for me to take her there myself!

Dorothy: Oh, will you? Could you? Oh ... but are you a clever enough wizard to manage it?

Wizard: Child ... you cut me to the quick! I'm an old Kansas man myself, born and bred in the heart of the Western wilderness. Premier balloonist par excellence of the Miracle Wonderland Carnival Company, until one day, while performing spectacular feats of stratospheric skill never before attempted by civilized man ... an unfortunate phenomena occurred. The balloon failed to return to the fair.

Lion: It did?

Wizard: Yes, there I was, floating through space, a man without a continent!

Dorothy: Weren't you frightened?

Wizard: Frightened? You are talking to a man who has laughed in the face of death ... sneered at doom ... and chuckled at catastrophe. I was petrified. Then suddenly the wind changed, and the balloon floated down into the heart of this noble city, where I was instantly acclaimed OZ, the First Wizard de Luxe!

Dorothy: Ohhh!

Wizard: Times being what they were, I accepted the job, retaining my balloon against the advent of a quick get-away. And in that balloon, my dear Dorothy, you and I will return to the land of E. Pluribus Unum!

—L. Frank Baum, *The Wizard of Oz*

You may recall that Toto ran off just as Dorothy was about to climb into the Wizard's balloon basket, and it sailed away without her. I always wondered where the Wizard went that day, and whether he ever got back home. It seemed to me the guy didn't really know where he was going. He just lived his life floating on the breeze and went wherever the balloon happened to touch down.

Are you drifting rather than consciously steering your life? Does the "balloon" decide where you will go? Instead of committing to the Lord and the unique and vital mission He has designed especially for us, we float around on the edge of the action, sometimes for years, sometimes forever. It's easier than steering our life deliberately and getting involved, but where will that take us?

Does this sound familiar? Do you know people who live with the "any road will do" mentality?

Alice: Would you tell me please which way I ought to go from here.

Cheshire Cat: That depends a good deal on where you want to get to.

Alice: I don't much care where.

Cheshire Cat: Then it doesn't matter which way you go, any road will get you there.

—Alice in Wonderland, Lewis Caroll

I can't live this way. I must have a path to follow. Over time it has become very clear to me that the gifts I've been given are far too valuable to waste irresponsibly. Shhh. Don't tell anyone, but I have been careless with some of my time already. Tick-tock, tick-tock.

When I think about the price Jesus and my parents paid to get me where I am today, I feel the weight and urgency of the mission I have to carry out. I require a clear course to follow and the finest navigation system to get me where I need to go—because I do need to go. I must find and carry out my mission.

Do you care where you go and how your precious gifts and time are spent? Well then, what's your mission? Instinctively, I think you know the direction. ❧

We must pay the most careful attention, therefore, to what we have heard, so that we do not drift away.

—Hebrews 2:1

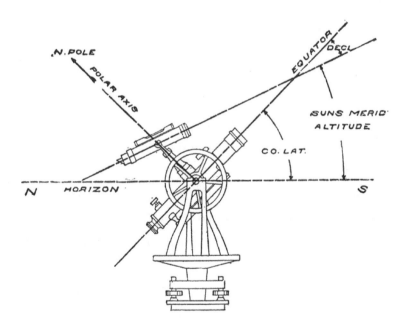

38

GLOBAL POSITIONING

"We can steer a course, but who's to set one?"
—Long John Silver in Treasure Island
Robert Louis Stevenson

ALL MODERN GPS DEVICES, or Global Positioning Systems, in planes, ships, cars, and even smartphones operate by relaying signals off satellites in space to tell you where you are and how to get where you need to go. The GPS will pinpoint your exact location and set your course in a straight line to your desired destination. The GPS will draw a true course to where you want to go. All you have to do is set the heading, then follow it exactly if you can. But guess what? No one can.

Rubbish, you say! Planes, boats, and cars all travel to and arrive at their desired destinations every day. That's true; however, they can never travel precisely on the course their GPS navigation has set for them. Depending on the vehicle and the skill of the driver, some will do better than others at staying on course, but none will travel precisely on course. Let me say it again: NONE.

Here's a simple example: You want to fly from Los Angeles to Honolulu. You set the heading of your GPS device in a straight line to Honolulu from LA, and away you go. That is how a GPS works, in a straight line from point A to point B. Eventually you will arrive at your intended destination.

Until you arrive in Honolulu, however, you will constantly be off course! Even though your GPS device has set a clear, straight-line course for you, it will be impossible for you to follow. In fact, never in the history of air and sea travel has anyone ever stayed precisely on course.....ever. Why? Because although the GPS is set in a straight line, it is simply not within the capability of any craft to resist completely the **way of the world.**

The world will throw things at your little craft. Whether you are piloting a plane or captaining a ship, you will be subject to the elements. Ocean currents and gusty winds are not the exception in travel; they are the rule. The lightest breeze can throw you slightly off. So, on your journey to Honolulu, try as you may, you cannot expect to execute a perfect voyage. This is unrealistic, because your vessel was not designed that way. You will always and regularly be pushed off course, even in excellent weather conditions. Forces are at work against you.

Therefore, your mission is not to stay perfectly on course. No, your mission is to regularly bring your vessel back on course so you can arrive at your destination. The proper navigation of any vessel is not the precise following of a straight line, but a state of constant correction in an attempt to follow a guideline.

Therefore, Go! ...with the expectation of being off course sometimes. It is normal. Set a true heading for your life and mission, and do your best to follow it. ❧

"Lady, you're about a half a bubble off plumb."
—Matthew Quigley in Quigley Down Under

Therefore, with minds that are alert and fully sober, set your hope on the grace to be brought to you when Jesus Christ is revealed at his coming."

—1 Peter 1:13

39

THE FLOUR SACK

"For the rest of his life, Oliver Twist remembers a single word of blessing spoken to him by another child because this word stood out so strikingly from the consistent discouragement around him."
—Charles Dickens, Oliver Twist

EDGAR TOOK CARE OF EFRAIM, right up until he went away. Every night, Edgar made sure his little brother had food and a warm place to sleep, if he could find them.

The cobbled lanes of the ancient Inca capital of Cuzco, Peru, are always full of tourists who buy cheap junk and give money to poor kids with sad faces. The brothers did all right, to be so young (only five and eight), without parents. They were going to make it. Safe. Together.

Then they took a job from the wrong man. Edgar was beaten and badly abused. While Efraim ran and hid like his brother told him, Edgar was knocked unconscious, tied in a flour sack, and tossed into the polluted Cuzco River. A woman down stream saw the bag move and thought it was a discarded dog. It was purely an accident when she discovered Edgar and saved his life.

It took Edgar a while to recover in the hospital, and by the time he went looking for his little brother, Efraim was starving and cold on the street. Yet they praised God the day they got each other back.

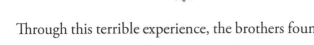

Through this terrible experience, the brothers found a home in our orphanage, and they are now thriving. How did that happen? ❧

"As the heavens are higher than the earth, so are my ways higher than your ways and my thoughts than your thoughts."

—Isaiah 55:9

40

OFF COURSE?

OES IT EVER DISCOURAGE YOU that even though you set your heading by accepting Christ, your walk with the Lord has not been going in a perfectly "Jesus-straight" line? Has it been a little off? Have you ever zigzagged, gone out of sync, even flipped out and gone "hog wild"? Have you ever felt that if the folks in church knew what you thought, did, or said in your private life they would think you were sinfully crazy?

Do you sometimes think you are a failure because you can't fly your life in a straight line? I hope you can relax a bit when I tell you that is an impossible dream. Try as you might, it is simply not within your capability to resist completely the *way of the world.*

Remember this well: "All have sinned and fall short of the glory of God" (Romans 3:23). Don't beat yourself up because you have drifted off course. This is a distraction and a waste of your time. It's going to happen because you were made that way. Get over it.

The trick is for:
your Christian navigation
   to alert you immediately
      when you have been diverted off course
         so that you can make a course correction
            and commit to regularly bringing your ship
               back on line

"I'll be back."

—The Terminator

Jesus set an example of a perfect navigational line to walk in this life. He walked it perfectly. Accepting Him as Lord and Savior is like setting our heading to attempt to walk that line beside Him. Christian people live in a state of constant correction, not in a state of perfection.

If you have a wobbly walk with Christ because the current is not running your way, do you think that excludes you from a role in missions? Caramba! Trust the navigation. Set it and have a little discipline to follow it. Follow it with your life, and don't get upset or distracted when you fail to walk a perfect line.

"Boy, a few dark clouds form on your horizon and you just go all to pieces, don't you?"

—Butch Cassidy and the Sundance Kid

Set your heading on Christ, the North Star that never moves, and keep coming back on course. That's all you have to do. Keep coming back. ❧

"Commit your way to the Lord; trust in him and he will do this."

—Psalm 37:5

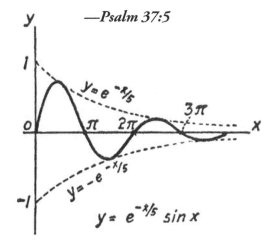

$$y = e^{-x/5} \sin x$$

121

41

THEREFORE, GO

Then Jesus came to them and said, "All authority in heaven and on earth has been given to me. Therefore go and make disciples of all nations, baptizing them in the name of the Father and of the Son and of the Holy Spirit, and teaching them to obey everything I have commanded you. And surely I am with you always, to the very end of the age."

—Matthew 28:18-20

EVERY CHRISTIAN, WITHOUT EXCEPTION, is a missionary—every one.

Read the above verses carefully. Note that Jesus did not say, "Therefore only pastors, seminary graduates, and highly educated Bible scholars GO ..." He was addressing every believing reader of the Bible. Every Christian is to GO and be a missionary for Christ somewhere, using whatever gifts and talents God has carefully woven together in them. That could mean GO down the street, GO across the nation, or GO around the world. It may just mean GO next door and visit with your neighbor or GO into the next room and talk to your wife or kids. But whatever you do, by God, you need to ,GO friends! And you are to be GOing every day that you wake up in the morning. You need to use the gifts He gave you in whatever way you can to share His message of salvation and build His Kingdom.

And remember the last line: "And surely I am with you always, to the very end of the age." Do not be afraid. You are not

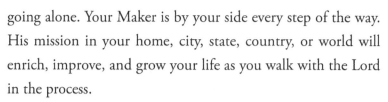

going alone. Your Maker is by your side every step of the way. His mission in your home, city, state, country, or world will enrich, improve, and grow your life as you walk with the Lord in the process.

Just listen for His call, and take the next step.

GO! This means YOU. 🪶

42

THE SKELETON

WALTER LOOKED LIKE A PRISONER from Auschwitz. He came to our orphanage with the same haunting expression artists sometimes try to capture when they're working on a horror movie. His dark eyes seemed to sink way back in his head, like chocolate chips pressed deep into cookie dough.

The boy recoiled in fear, even when the other children came near. He wouldn't have anything to do with adults, even if they were trying to help. Trust was long gone. The skin hung off his twelve-year-old frame like a cheap suit on a frail old man. Starvation had been one of his many constant companions.

Walter had scars, too. Somebody had burned him with hot water or grease or something. I really thought he was past the point of no return, beyond physical and emotional repair. However, the love of Christ in all its many forms is truly amazing.

I barely recognize Walter today. His gaunt cheeks have filled in, and the occasional smile even flashes across his face. It took a while though.

We didn't just visit an orphanage. We lived there. Those kids are not just somebody's kids who were hurt and discarded. They're ours forever. We became their parents. In any form or fashion, working with kids and helping them grow in the Lord is as worthwhile a mission as there is. Give it try but beware, it will change your self-centered life forever. ❧

"And whosoever shall offend one of these little ones that believe in me, it is better for him that a millstone were hanged about his neck, and he were cast into the sea."

—Mark 9:24, kjv

ANY PROFITS ARISING FROM THE SALE OF THIS LITTLE WORK, WILL BE DEVOTED TO THE BENEFIT OF The Orphans of St. Philomena's Asylum, ATTACHED TO THE INSTITUTION OF ST. JOSEPH'S, NEAR EMMITTSBURG, MARYLAND.

43

NO ESCAPE

Sgt. O'Neill: "Bob, I got a bad feeling on this one, all right? I mean, I got a bad feeling. I don't think I'm gonna make it out of here. You understand what I'm saying to you?"
Sgt. Barnes: "Everybody's got to die sometime, Red."

—Platoon

IHAVE SEEN DEAD FOLKS from time to time. Not like what soldiers see in war or anything like that, but I've seen it happen a fair bit. Let's put it this way: I've seen the face of death enough to know that it really does happen to people. And every time I see or get near death, I am reminded of my physical death and wonder what bus I'm going to take afterward.

For many years, my reaction to death was to get away from it fast and forget it. Like Woodrow Call in Lonesome Dove, my view was, "The best thing you can do for death is ride off from it." I did that for a very long time. I ran.

But hard as you try, you can never run far enough away, can you? Why do we tend to put our own death so far back in the remote corners of our mind and try to ignore it? Do we really think we'll be the first to avoid this reality? Stop fooling yourself. This day will arrive for all of us. ❧

"No one here gets out alive."

—The Doors

44

REASON #1 FOR MISSIONS

"The only hope you have is to accept the fact that you're already dead. The sooner you accept that, the sooner you'll be able to function as a soldier is supposed to function."

—Lt. Colonel Ronald C. Speirs in Band of Brothers

I AM GOING TO DIE.

Yep, I've come to terms. If you're willing to let go, this wild notion can be liberating. They say if you can convince a soldier in battle there is no way out and he is already physically dead, he will fight better than any other soldier trying to save his own skin. Let me give you some good news: You're already dead, so you're free to act like it.

For years I only looked upon my death as a distant possibility way down the line. I thought, "It could maybe happen." I was very disconnected with my mortality. I had too much to do.

"When we attempt to imagine death, we perceive ourselves as spectators."

—Sigmund Freud

If you think this way, don't feel alone.

I have a lawyer friend who works for a lot of rich guys and writes up documents like business contracts, partnership agreements, powers of attorney, trust funds, and wills. He once expressed astonishment that so many people did not actually

believe they were going to die. He laughed out loud when he told me the key thing: "The richer the guy, the less he thinks he's going to die."

When my friend drafts a will for a client, almost invariably rich "Mr. In-Control" will begin to dictate the wording like this: "If I die, I want this money to go here, and that property to go there, the kids get this, the ex-wives get that," and so on. Then the lawyer politely stops him and says, "I'm sorry, I can't write it up that way."

Offended, the client says, "Why not? That's the way I want it!"

The lawyer replies, "Because your will cannot read 'if I die.' The proper wording is, 'when I die.' This thing is actually going to happen to you. You don't get to keep the ranch, the plane, the American Express card, or even your underwear. You will not retain control of anything you have bought, built or currently manage. You're out of this picture forever."

"You have made my days a mere handbreadth; The span of my years is as nothing before you, Everyone is but a breath, even those who seem secure."

—Psalm 39: 5

The sooner we all get that, the better off we'll be. No matter what battles we've been winning here on earth, we are going to die and leave everything behind. None of our possessions, accomplishments, or perceived glory on this earth will be coming with us.

Can you handle that? ❧

> "For over a thousand years Roman conquerors returning from the wars enjoyed the honor of triumph, a tumultuous parade. In the procession came trumpeters, musicians and strange animals from the conquered territories, together with carts laden with treasure and captured armaments. The conquerors rode in a triumphal chariot, the dazed prisoners walking in chains before him. Sometimes his children robed in white stood with him in the chariot, or rode the trace horses. A slave stood behind the conqueror, holding a golden crown and whispering in his ear a warning: that all glory is fleeting."
>
> **—closing lines of the movie Patton**

45

DEATH AROUND ME

"My! People come and go so quickly here!"
—Dorothy Gale in *The Wizard of Oz*

T STARTED WITH MY DOG, Mojo, and my brother's mouse, Henry. They died, and I never saw them again.

My step-grandfather, George, attended the Naval Academy and had a beautiful farm in Virginia. We rode horses together, and he taught me about lawn mowers, how to gut a fish, how to dress sharp, and how to clean up a bathroom when I was finished using it. One day I told my granddad how nice I thought it must be to own a farm like that. He stopped, looked me dead in the eye, and said, "We're not owners here, Stevie, just caretakers. Sometimes we think we own things, but we don't." I thought about what Granddaddy George said some years later when he told me good-bye in the hospital. "We're just caretakers." I never saw him again.

Uncle Coy rode my brother's bicycle when he was eighty-six. Great-Gram screamed he'd break every bone in his body, but he didn't care. He had a blast. Uncle Coy was the funniest old person I ever knew. He could puff on his cigar and blow a smoke ring across the room. He got his legs amputated, and Great-Gram lost her marbles. They both died and I never saw them again.

Coach Hanagriff was my eighth-grade history teacher. He had a heart condition and threatened that if we were bad in class, he was going to throw one of his nitroglycerin pills at us. The students had to wear coats and ties to his funeral. My friend Kenny was with me, and we couldn't help nervously giggling at each other. But when we walked up front and I got one good look at Coach's gray face in the casket, my mirth was about as dead as he was. It was real. We never saw Coach again.

Leonard was my dad's buddy and liked to plant azaleas. He taught me a lot about gardening. We went to his farm sometimes and rode on the tractor. I came home from school one day and found out he had flipped that tractor over into a lake on his farm. I never saw him again.

IN MEMORIAM

In Memory of
BILLIE MOURET
WHO PASSED AWAY JAN. 3, 1936
Her charming ways and smiling face
Are a pleasure to recall;
She had a kindly word for each,
And died beloved by all.
MOM AND AUNT.

Uncle John was a lovable character who was deeply ingrained in my life. His pipe tobacco gave off the most pleasant aroma. He liked to laugh, play tennis, and drink whiskey. He was about seventy when he went to the dentist one day and the guy saw something in his mouth. The next thing I knew he was getting chemotherapy. Six months later Uncle John was gone. I really loved him, and I never saw him again.

All these observations lead me to conclude that one day soon, you're never going to see me again. My reaction to death today is not to run, but to hear the tick-tock of the clock and realize my time to serve the Lord here on earth is limited.

They say death speaks to us. What's it telling you? ❧

"So teach us to number our days, that we may gain a heart of wisdom."

—Psalm 90:12

46

THE MIST

"And just like that, she was gone."

—Forrest Gump

I ONCE DATED A GIRL whose wealthy family lived in a mansion. They are precious Christian people whom I love with all my heart. Her dad was a larger-than-life lawyer and former pro football player.

Ed had it all. He had a powerful presence, crackled with energy, and had a beautiful wife, four gorgeous daughters, and a baby boy. He had lots of people working for him. I liked him instantly, because he was adventurous. He hunted, fished, and climbed mountains. The first time I met him, he told me about climbing Mount Kilimanjaro. Ed had a warm way and a broad smile, and I very much looked forward to getting to know him.

He went to climb Grand Teton in Wyoming with some friends shortly after we met. He left on Wednesday and came back on Sunday, in a casket.

Something had gone wrong with his climb, a faulty harness or something, and that was that. His gate made the boarding call, and he caught his flight up to heaven. No prior notice, no delay, no changing airlines, no chance to call home. Period. Done.

My brief encounter with this good man, the way he came into and went out of my life so fast, spoke to me more than anyone can possibly imagine. It was truly a "here today, gone tomorrow" relationship. I am quite sure this dramatic event spoke to hundreds of people in a multitude of ways, and there's no telling how God shaped their hearts and minds through it. As for me, I'll bet Ed would never have guessed in a million years that he would one day become one of the reasons I decided to work in missions.

God used Ed to get to get my attention. Who's He using to get yours? ❧

"You do not even know what will happen tomorrow. What is your life? You are a mist that appears for a little while and then vanishes."

—James 4:14

47

REASON #2 FOR MISSIONS

"They are not of the world, even as I am not of it."

—John 17:16

I DON'T LIVE HERE.

If you can buy in completely that you are actually going to die, and you can buy the eternal life message of the Bible, then it seems to me you need to buy into the idea that planet Earth is not your permanent home. You do not live here. Never did. Never will. It's temporary. You are just a visitor in this place. You have been sent on a mission to this place.

Think of it in earthly terms: I once went to Grand Cayman for a week. I went swimming. I ate lobster. I breathed, slept, and saw the sunset. I did a lot of stuff there and met lots of people. Walking on the beach was fun, but wrecking my moped was not so fun. I had good and bad experiences and lessons. I was alive in Cayman, but I was not from there and I did not live there. My earthly home was in Texas, and a week later I went "home."

That is the snapshot I see of my life here on Earth. I'm a visitor on a mission to this planet. I am alive here, I have experiences here, but this is not home.

"….live out your time as foreigners here…."

—1 Peter 1:17

Oh, and get this crazy twist: I don't know how long this mission to Earth is going to last.

In Cayman, I had booked a reservation to come home in a week. My excursion to Earth is on an "open ticket." I know I'm going home, but I don't know when. What travel agent booked this strange trip, anyway? My flight could be called at any moment, or fifty years from now.

They say our God is a God of order, but He would be fired from most earthly travel companies I know. Indefinite standby does not make travelers feel secure, but standby is precisely where we are on this journey of life. You don't travel home until you are called.

So, I have left home, right now I am on a mission to another place called Earth, and I will be catching my flight back home … sooner or later. It is as simple as that.

> *"…our citizenship is in Heaven…"*
> **—Philippians 3:20**

Note: Whenever I leave home, the people who love me always give me instructions and advice: "Be careful, mind your manners, stay out of danger, don't take chances, stay away from unsavory characters, pay attention, watch what you're doing, etc." My wife and girls do that with me, as did my parents before them.

I keep firmly in mind that my Father in heaven loves me very much, and He has given me instructions as well. A Bible is within my easy reach, and when I read it, God tells me all those things I need to know for protection and productivity on this mission to Earth. The Bible is my instruction manual. Prayer is when I call home. Have you called in lately? ❧

"This is Mork calling Orsen. Come in Orsen"

—Robin Williams in Mork and Mindy

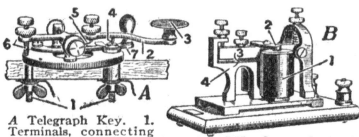

A Telegraph Key. 1. Terminals, connecting the ends of a break in the line wire ; 2 Key Lever, depressed by its Button (3), thus closing the circuit through the platinum Points (4). When not in use, the Spring (5) holds up 2, which then rests on its Back Stop (6), the break being closed by setting the Lever (7) in the position shown. B Sounder. Currents through the Magnet (1) cause it to draw down its Armature (2), which brings the Stop (3) against the Anvil (4) with a click for each current passing.

48

I WILL NOT FEAR

THINK ABOUT THESE POETIC WORDS from the King James Bible for a moment, and let them really sink in: "Yea, though I walk through the valley of the shadow of death, I will fear no evil: for thou art with me" (Psalm 23:4).

These are very bold words which can be hard to remember sometimes when you are faced with the possibly of sudden death. I think back to times when the end seemed imminent, and each time led me closer to God and the urgency of accepting my mission assignment. I think He is always trying to get our attention for that very reason. He wants us to get involved with the gifts we've received and the experiences we've had in our life.

Has death ever brushed your shoulder? It will sooner or later, but don't be afraid. Rest in the certainty that our Father is with us daily. This regular practice of resting in Him will help you to be brave each day, especially on the big day when death comes knocking. ❧

Mama, take this badge off of me.
I can't use it anymore.
It's gettin' dark, too dark to see.
I feel like I'm knockin' on heaven's door.

—Bob Dylan

49

A FEVER PITCH

"Boys, I realize that some of us are not going to finish this journey. Cherrie, I want you and Kermit to go on. You can get out. I will stop here."

—Theodore Roosevelt, stricken with malaria, ordering his team to leave him behind for dead along the River of Doubt in Brazil

CONTRACTED MALARIA in the Amazon jungle. The freight train hit me, and I plunged toward death about two weeks later in Cali, Colombia. I didn't know what it was except from what I saw in movies about the British army and the people who built the Panama Canal. The way it works is weird. A mosquito bites you and puts a parasite in your blood. It hides in your liver to multiply during the gestation period. You don't know what has happened, and you feel normal. The parasite population in your liver grows, and eventually they decide to have a big party. You have what's called a liver cycle, and the creatures run wild all through your bloodstream. Your temperature fires up full throttle to fight the intruders in an epic battle for your very life.

At the time of the event, and trust me when I tell you it was

an event, I was having a spirited discussion on a rooftop patio with my Colombian host about Teddy Roosevelt's hostile takeover of the Isthmus of Panama. I'd just learned Teddy had snatched the prime real estate when our country couldn't agree with Colombia on a sale price. It was the quickest the US had ever recognized the sovereignty of a new nation. Battleships were reportedly there the next day, Panama was born, and T. R. completed his canal.

A shock wave of chills knocked me out of my chair. I mumbled to my stunned host as I got up and ran to my room. I jumped fully clothed into the bed and pulled the blankets over me. They say I babbled incoherently as my muscles convulsed and contracted. I shivered and hallucinated for over two hours before the fever broke, and I sweated right through my clothes and sheets. My host family told me the next day that I must know God, because I spoke to Him all night.

Though I walk through the valley of the shadow of death, I shall fear no evil. The author of all things watches over me. And I have a fine horse.

—Mattie Ross in True Grit (2010)

The good news was malaria and dengue fever are so common in Colombia that there are free clinics to get treatment. The bad news was this was Thursday and the clinic didn't open until the following Tuesday. "No hay problema, señor!" they said. "You probably won't die by then."

I did eventually get treatment and got well, but let me tell you something, in those few days I learned what it's like to die of malaria. It fools you unmercifully. The fever goes away, you rest, feel better, and you think maybe it's gone. Then the fever comes back, and with each fever event the temperature gets hotter as your body tries to fight the intruders. You begin to live in mortal fear of the fever returning, and when it does, you feel your organs and brain overheating. You don't die of the parasite itself. You actually cook to death as your body tries to fight it. You're killed by the slow-roasting fever of your own immune system.

I spoke with God many times in those terrible days. I thank Him regularly to this day for the chloroquine phosphate that saved my life. I walked into Colombia thinking, "What am I going to get?" I walked out thinking, "What can I give other people with the time I have left?"

Anything like this ever happen to you? ❧

"When someone is diagnosed with cancer, why does their perspective suddenly change?"

—Tom Laughlin

50

SWALLOWED BY THE SEA

"'I love you,' I whispered into the ear of the ocean. 'Ever since I've known you, I have loved you. I must see all of your marvels, know all your beauty.' And the ocean listened, and snuggled still closer to me."

—Wade Hughes

I'VE HAD A LIFELONG LOVE AFFAIR with the ocean, and guiding dive tours in the Galapagos Islands was like getting married to her. No matter how time and distance have separated us, I am bonded to this lover forever. I communicated more actively with God while I was soaking up every moment in this remote and remarkable corner of the world. It's that kind of a place.

A mid-Pacific archipelago, Galapagos is a magnet for majestic sea animals and multitudes of other creatures. The Humboldt is a deep, frigid undersea current that streams north from Antarctica, up the coast of Chile, hangs a left at Peru, and pumps out into the middle of the ocean. It impacts the mountainous Galapagos Islands at the sea floor, forcing it into what's called an "upwelling." Nutrient-rich water jets to the surface around the islands like a wellspring, bringing small fish, sea lions, sea turtles, birds, big fish, and so on. It's an exciting food-chain dance every day, which allows scuba divers to view large schools of marine wildlife. This unique location is arguably the very best theater in the world to view this kind of gigantic show.

"The sea, once it casts its spell, holds one in its net of wonder forever."

—Jacques-Yves Cousteau

Not for the beginner. The Humboldt along with other intersecting mid-Pacific currents also make this one of the most unpredictable and dangerous places for scuba diving in the world. Though right on the equator, Galapagos is not calm, clear Caribbean water. The deep ocean is constantly swirling around and changing the dive conditions. The water temperature is cold, and visibility underwater can sometime be very poor. The surface can suddenly become treacherous. It all plays a role in how you plan and execute a dive. Thick wet suits with hoods, gloves, and booties are standard gear.

I guided a group of underwater photographers on a three-week dive tour exploring the northern islands, Darwin and Wolf, far out in the middle of nowhere. The largest schools of hammerhead sharks on earth are located there. Each roughly the size of a Cadillac, these prehistoric monsters run in packs that number in the hundreds.

We anchored late afternoon in one of the few protected sites in this remote area, the cove at Wolf Island. The bay has a large mouth where the sea glides in and out freely, but is a well-protected harbor, safe from the turbulent Pacific. The sun went down, and the crew made a beautiful supper of grilled tuna on the back deck. I was planning to turn in early when one of the clients suggested a night dive. A small group of six divers responded enthusiastically. I checked safety conditions. The night was clear, with no wind; all was very quiet. I agreed we were a go and conducted a simple orientation of the dive plan onboard.

Bobbing on the surface, everyone gave the okay signal. We descended to the sea floor, and a slight ebb and flow softly slid the team back and forth, their flashlights doing a little dance around. Again, all gave the okay sign, and I gave them the signal to proceed along the bottom in the direction of the bay wall for viewing nocturnal coral and anemones. They broke into pairs with their cameras, and I accompanied off to the side so as not to disturb their photos. We covered the sixty or seventy yards to the side of the bay, and I remember shining my flashlight at the wall when I got within twenty feet. The sand at the base of the wall stirred slightly, but I sensed no danger. We proceeded to examine the coral and sea creatures up close.

Nothing happened until I crept within about three feet of the wall where ocean swell met solid, unyielding rock. The violent currents swirling there were undetectable, and much of the next five minutes was a panicked blur. The ocean snatched me without warning and shook me like a rag doll. I was spinning helplessly in its ferocious grip, slamming against the wall. Upside down, round and round—I didn't know which way was up. My mask was gone, my regulator was out of my mouth, and my flashlight dangled from the lanyard on my wrist. Disoriented and frightened are understatements; no words can describe the terror I felt. In my mind I could hear my instructor's steady voice as my left arm patiently swept out in the regulator recovery technique for which I'd been so thoroughly drilled. It wasn't working. I couldn't find my air hose, I couldn't see, I couldn't breathe, I was in sixty feet of water at night, and the Wolf Island washing machine had me on spin cycle.

My heart throbbed in my chest, and panic was headed my way. I was being swallowed by the sea. Even if I had known which way to swim for the surface, I was already so suffocated

that I would probably pass out and drown before I got there. So I made a desperate move.

The only control at my disposal was the inflator button on my buoyancy compensator vest. It was the only chance I had, but it would put me at high risk of getting damaged or even killed. Picture shaking up a

can of Coca-Cola and then popping the top off. That gives you some idea of what happens with dissolved nitrogen in your body when you breathe compressed air at depth and then race to the surface. It's called decompression sickness, or more commonly, "the bends."

I didn't have a choice, and my time was running out fast. Death from drowning was moments away, and what might happen was irrelevant. I squeezed the button and filled the vest with air to capacity. At the same time I exhaled continuously so my lungs wouldn't explode and rocketed to the surface.

"And I'm gonna be high as a kite by then."
—Elton John - Rocket Man

My head popped above the sea, gasping and choking the salty water out of my throat, and I slowly stabilized. The bay was just as I'd left it: calm, quiet, with only a gentle sway of the ocean, back and forth, back and forth. Weird. I wondered what had happened to my team. Were they okay?

They all broke the surface one by one, coughing, screaming, and crying. Not one had a mask on, and some of their lights, cameras, and even fins were gone, snatched by the ocean. They were terrified and really unhappy. Stevie the Guide did not have an answer for the dive team when they asked why I hadn't foreseen the perils of Wolf Island.

Report card on protecting our valued clients: Failed. The tour company headquarters in Quito gave me a hard time about it when the incident was reported. I just felt lucky to be alive.

My respect for the ocean and the Lord's control over everything went up a notch after that. No matter how in charge or in control I think I am, He can show me who's boss very quickly. Just like my parents when I was a boy, God can call me home whenever He wants.

Has God ever shown you just how small you are? ❧

"Watch your step when you enter God's House. Enter to Learn."

—Ecclesiastes 5:1

145

51

REASON #3 FOR MISSIONS

I WILL MEET JESUS CHRIST face-to-face.

We have to go and actually meet God. The Bible says, "We must all appear before the judgment seat of Christ, so that each of us may receive what is due us for the things done while in the body, whether good or bad" (2 Corinthians 5:10).

Judgment Day, dude! Yikes!

If that verse doesn't blow your hair back, I'm not sure what will. The divine appointment is every bit as certain as your death and departure from earth. I don't believe there's a waiting room; it happens on the same day in the same moment. Wow! As my Dad would say,

"You'd better take a close look at that."

The King, The Father, the Alpha and Omega, the head honcho, the big enchilada. We're all going to meet Him personally, and He's going to judge us. What will that day be like? Being of Earthly training, I think of lofty courtroom situations in which I might find myself in front of the bench here on the planet. I don't mean to make light of the situation;, this is just the way my mind works, the way He made me. I wonder about it.

Sometimes I think it will be like visiting the king of England during medieval times. I walk through a giant set of doors, and guards in suits of armor snap to attention. In a loud voice some lieutenant way down the corridor cries out, "His Majesty the King will see you now!"

This could be freaky. Am I going to need a lawyer? Will I be ready to meet God? Will He know me? Silly question. Will I just pass out on the floor at the sight of God, like the Cowardly Lion meeting the Wizard?

"I am Oz, the great and powerful. Who are you?!"
—The Wizard of Oz

I hope I don't get confused and not understand what to do. Will there be someone to greet me when I get there and show me the ropes before I go into the throne room and make a fool of myself?

"An escort from his way station gets a signal.
He goes down and waits for the outcome.
If the guy lives, the escort wasted a trip.
If the guy dies, the escort takes him back to his way station
He puts him in line for his final destination.
You follow?"
—Joe Pendleton in Heaven Can Wait

And are there any special rules or proper etiquette I have to follow when granted a private audience with the Creator of the Universe? Will my escort teach me these things?

"Now it's all highly ritualized, of course. You may look at him,
but do not speak unless spoken to. If he stands, you must bow. If
he bows, you bow lower. Do I look presentable?"
—Simon Graham in The Last Samurai

I like to think when I meet God, it will be like when I would arrive home as a small child. I will burst through the door, and the first thing I will do is run screaming with joy to find my Dad, the Lord of the Manor. When I locate Him I'll jump up in His lap and hug and kiss Him with all my strength. I will cry at how happy I am to see Him, and He will be just as happy to see me. He will hug me and tell me how much He loves me. It will be a wonderful homecoming.

But there's always that element of human doubt, isn't there? We don't really know, do we?

Whatever that incredible day is all about, I have surrendered to the certainty that I'll be there. God and me. Face-to-face.

It could happen tomorrow. Are you ready for this? Who will show you the way and speak on your behalf when you get there?

"My dear children, I write this to you so that you will not sin. But if anybody does sin, we have an advocate with the Father— Jesus Christ, the Righteous One.

—1 John 2:1

If anybody does sin…?

Hmmmm….

You haven't…have you?

52

KRYPTONIC TRAJECTORY

"Last night I saw an accident, on the corner of Third and Green.
Two cars collided and I got excited, just being part of that scene.
It was Mrs. Tom Walker and her beautiful daughter,
Pamela was driving the car.
They got hit by a man in a light blue sedan
Who had obviously been to a bar.
And they don't know how lucky they are."

—John Prine, "The Accident"

I FLEW OVER THREE CARS the week before my twenty-first birthday.

You'd have to have been there to understand what a miracle it was I survived almost completely unscathed. In a sense, I wasn't there either because it happened so instantaneously. I don't remember much of the actual event. Please forgive the comparison, but do you remember the story of Superman? He was placed as a baby in an escape rocket and safely launched off the planet Krypton by his loving parents, just before the place exploded and was blown to smithereens. It was sort of like that.

"Faster than a speeding bullet, more powerful than a locomotive,
able to leap tall buildings in a single bound."

—DC Comics

I was sitting on the right rear fender well in the back of an open Chevy pickup, telling a story to my friend Tom, who sat on the other fender well. I gesture with my hands when I talk, so I wasn't holding onto the side rail. The police officer later told me, had I been holding on, I might have died or been crippled for life that day. Weird.

There I was, spinning a big tale for Tom, when I momentarily turned forward to look over the cab of the truck in the direction we were speeding. Wind in my hair, that's the last thing I remember, but Tom helped me piece it together afterward.

He said I was telling him a funny story, and we were both laughing. I looked to my right toward the front of our truck. For a moment, I turned back to Tom as if to continue the story, then I looked forward again and my eyes "got real big." Tom said when I turned back to him for the second time he knew something was wrong.

"Steve," he said. "I didn't know what it was, but the look of horror on your face said it all. I tightened my grip on the side rail of the truck," Tom went on, "because I knew something bad was about to happen just by your expression. Along with your face, I saw your hands race down, reaching for the side rail, and then you were gone, just like that. You instantly vanished when I heard and felt the crash."

I have the briefest memory of flying through the air, followed by a whoosh of air next to my left ear. I remember no impact or pain whatsoever, then silence for the longest time after that. It was really peaceful. One moment I was talking to Tom in the truck, the next I was walking down the road under a highway overpass all by myself. It was instantaneous. There was no one around, and it seemed really quiet and dreamlike.

A couple came running up to me. The man's face was ashen, and the woman was crying hysterically. "Oh my God! Are you all right?!" they both seemed to scream in unison as they began checking me out in horrified disbelief. I sympathized over their panic, but in my state of blissful shock, I felt fine.

"I'm okay," I said, not knowing what they were talking about. "Are you okay?" Seemed like the proper response at the time.

"Oh my God, we thought we killed you!" They kept looking at me as if I were a ghost, repeatedly checking my head and neck. It was then I noticed I had some scrapes on my hands. "What happened?" I asked feebly. That's when they gently turned me around so I could see and understand.

The total mayhem of the four-car accident some fifty yards away hit me like a brick. Our truck ran a red light just as the traffic on the freeway service road was driving through. We broadsided a Riviera at the same moment a small truck and a Ford LTD pummeled into our left side. The streetlight post was sheared off and lying on the ground, while smoke from the wreckage was filling the overpass. Glass, car parts, and debris were strewn everywhere, bleeding people were wandering around dazed or lay crying in the street, and a crowd was gathering.

"We just missed hitting all that," the crying woman said, pointing to the black Suburban parked just to the right a little inside the overpass. "Then we saw you! You flew out of that yellow truck with your body stretched out and arms in front like Superman, and you came at our car like a speeding bullet. We swerved to miss hitting you in midair, but you went down by our right tire and we thought we had run over your head."

That was the whoosh of air I remember feeling. Their truck tire had passed within an inch or so of my face.

"Caution: Cape does not enable user to fly."

—Batman costume warning label, WAL-MART, 1995

Every single person in that accident was hospitalized except me. I was checked and released. The police at the scene said my long flight had used up all the energy of the impact, so by the time I touched down on the pavement I wasn't going very fast. Had I been holding on, I likely would have hit the back of the cab instead of flying over the cab and two cars, on course for a safe landing.

I should have been badly injured or killed. There is no explanation to me other than God plucked me out of danger. It made me start asking why. Why did He do it? Did He have some other plans for me? Why am I here? The questions just keep growing with each day of my life. What does He want with me? What is my mission?

Did you ever feel like the Lord shielded you from harm? ❦

"He will cover you with his feathers, and under His wings you will find refuge."

—Psalm 91:4

53

SO UNTIL THEN

Ben Gates: "What was his secret?"
John Gates: "A treasure! A treasure beyond all imagining."

—National Treasure

LET'S ROLE-PLAY A LITTLE, shall we?

You've croaked, kicked the bucket, gone out for the long ball, and are now pushing up daisies. It doesn't matter how it happened, you have now gone from earth. "Ladies and gentlemen, Elvis has left the building!"

Now then, poof! You are talking with the Creator of the Universe, just you and Him. That's gotta feel different. So, what do you say to God Almighty after life as you've known it has just been snuffed out and you stand in front of the pearly gates? Seems like that would put you a little off balance, wouldn't it? "Hey there … er … how's your day going, uh, sir? Nice place ya have here." What could you possibly say?

More importantly, when you get there, what is God going to say to you? I really hope God gives me a fatherly bear hug and says to me, "Well done, My good and faithful servant!"

That's what I want! Clang the bell, baby! Hooray for our side! I always liked the distinction of a person graduating with honors. That's what this sounds like to me when our Maker acknowledges the way we used our free will on earth. "Atta boy, My son! Way to go!" Would that feel great, or what?

So, how can we live our lives so that God might bestow on us those most beautiful of all lines? Here are two clues from the Bible:

"Do not store up for yourselves treasures on earth, where moths and vermin destroy, and where thieves break in and steal. But store up for yourselves treasures in heaven.... For where your treasure is, there your heart will be also."

—Matthew 6:19-21

Truly a treasure we can't possibly imagine............
It also says:

"What good is it, my brothers and sisters, if someone claims to have faith but has no deeds? Can such faith save them? Suppose a brother or a sister is without clothes and daily food. If one of you says to them, "Go in peace; keep warm and well fed," but does nothing about their physical needs, what good is it? In the same way, faith by itself, if it is not accompanied by action, is dead."

—James 2:14-17

We cannot use our works to buy a ticket to heaven. We already received a very expensive ticket free of charge. I've got mine. Have you got yours? (If not, "You'd better take a close look at that.")

However, now that we have this amazing free gift, my works honor the One who gave it to me. We serve the physical needs of people, share the love of Christ, and help them to receive this free gift as well.

That's why I do missions. Right there. 🪶

"We love because He loves us."

—Max Lucado

"A bell's not a bell 'til you ring it. A song's not a song 'til you sing it. Love in your heart wasn't put there to stay. Love isn't love 'til you give it away!"

—Oscar Hammerstein II

54

THE GANGSTER

"You can get more with a kind word and a gun than you can with just a kind word."

—Al Capone

HUGO REFUSED TO GO to a children's home in Cuzco. Life on the street was manageable and free of too many rules. At age eight, he didn't trust adults anyway. Hugo sold trinkets to tourists, slept in a flophouse, and didn't have to go to school. He ran the show, but our friends at the orphanage kept working with him. Purely out of physical need, Hugo surrendered one day and took a bunk in a place where he learned about the Lord. But he didn't like it at first.

Hugo fought the system like a rabid dog. He was often physically and ver-

bally abusive to the staff and other kids. He did not want to be there.

The orphanage learned that Hugo had a dream: He was going to be an American-style gangster. He had seen old movies about John Dillinger, Baby Face Nelson, and Al Capone. He was seduced by the power of the tommy gun and the flash of pin-striped suits. Nobody mistreated these guys the way Hugo had been mistreated. A gangster doesn't have to rely on anyone, and takes whatever he wants. No one would ever bother Hugo again.

Hugo advanced in school, and after a while his dream changed: He decided to become a lawyer. It was beautiful! He had it all figured out. He could avoid danger, wear the pin-striped suits, and have the power to steal from people legally!

As time went by, however, Hugo gradually realized his many blessings, went to church, and studied Scripture with his new family. The orphanage director, my large friend Jeremy, is kind, gentle, but very firm with these boys. He dragged Hugo back into class often, put him on restriction, and made him clean toilets. He taught Hugo competitive sports and showed him the value of clean clothes, a well-made bed, and a daily hot shower. The man Hugo once hated and dreamed of killing with a machine gun became a father he loved with all his heart. Eventually, Hugo accepted Christ, was baptized, and with more time developed a new vision for his God-given mission.

Today Hugo is a Christian lawyer fighting for the rights of orphaned, abandoned, and neglected children in Peru. He teaches English and Christian studies. Hugo is our friend, and we thank God for his life.

Want to meet him and our other kids? Just tell us when to arrange a mission for you to Cuzco. ❧

"Therefore, if anyone is in Christ, he is a new creation. The old has passed away; behold, the new has come."

—2 Corinthians 5:17

55

YOUR KIDS' MISSIONS?

"I believe the children are our future
Teach them well and let them lead the way.
Show them all the beauty they possess inside.
Give them a sense of pride to make it easier.
Let the children's laughter remind us how we used to be."

—Michael Masser and Linda Creed, "The Greatest Love of All"

I DON'T HAVE THE TIME or space to tell you about all the young people we have served and helped to serve in the mission field. The things young people have done to serve God on short-term trips—soccer clinics, music ministry, medical ministry, art, construction, vacation Bible school, the Awana program, teaching, etc.—are too numerous and varied to cover here. But I can tell you about my girls.

Ellie was twelve and Martha Anne was eight when we moved to Peru for four years to serve in missions. We knew they would have to learn Spanish and the ways of a completely different culture. We knew it would be hard for them to leave family, friends, and all that was familiar. Tears were going to be included; this was a given. They worked with the new environment God gave them. I was especially proud of the way they blew past my basic Spanish on their way to fluency. They are to me the real heroes of our amazing journey into missions.

I did not foresee some of the other things they got in the field. It may take them years to realize the treasures they've acquired from living and serving abroad.

One treasure is that they dealt directly with adults on visiting teams. Because these were often the only visitors who spoke English, the girls were happy to play and interact with adults. So they have developed a level of respect and comfort with older people. This is very evident now that we are back in the States.

Another treasure is that our girls served equally on every type of mission you can think of. They served as receptionists in clinics, assisted doctors, fitted people with eyeglasses, and helped draw blood. They served as translators and facilitators for all kinds of projects, and acted as liaisons between team members and orphanage staff.

Cuzco, Peru, is a very international place, and the girls not only learned Spanish and Quechua culture, but got exposed to pretty much every other culture on this planet. They have spoken a little or a lot with people from Asia, Australia, the Middle East, Scandinavia, the South Pacific, Russia, and other parts of the world.

In my opinion, time away from the USA, technology, and a fast pace is healthy for young people. In Peru, we lived in a culture where few people knew what texting was or even had access to a computer, let alone the World Wide Web. It made my kids more grounded, and exposure to real poverty helped them realize the amazing blessings we have here in our country. Many are the times they have visited one-room adobe homes with a dirt floor, fireplace in the middle, and guinea pigs running around underfoot. They know what it is to be materially poor.

Most of all, Ellie and Martha Anne saw firsthand and got involved with the world of active missionary service. They themselves have worked very hard at serving the Lord and sharing the love of Christ with folks who need it. They now know the importance, and what it's all about.

One of our best friends in Peru is Gabriella. She is beautiful, and speaks English, Spanish, Quechua, and maybe another language or three. "Ella" aspires to be a missionary doctor and could be whatever she pursues.

Whatever it is, rest assured she will share the gospel of Christ with her every breath. You wouldn't know it to meet her, but she was a neglected, abandoned child. Had she not been one of the lucky ones picked up by the El Arca Orphanage, Ella likely would have died or been enslaved.

Our girls have heard the stories of their friends, the kids we serve. They read and memorize Scripture and know firsthand why we do what we do.

Would it benefit your kids to have a little of that? ❧

"Start children off on the way they should go, and even when they are old they will not turn from it."

—Proverbs 22:6

56

TOUCH ME

"How we work and for whom we work really matters."
—Steve Corbett and Brian Fikkert, When Helping Hurts

E SOMETIMES THINK, in our paternalistic, godlike American mentalities, it is we who are doing all the giving and bestowing of blessing upon the poor, unwashed masses. We think sometimes if we can give something, or build something, or teach something, the materially poor will be enriched by our reaching out to them with our abundant gifts.

Often, we are fools full of ourselves.

Those who participate in missions know all too well that when we come home to the safety of the US from the far corners of the world, most often it is we who have received the truckload of transformational treasure. We return with fresh new perspective to share. We feel blessed and different. Our focus is turned outward.

God touches us, just like He touches those we serve, and we all go home changed.

But the Master comes, and the foolish crowd
Never can quite understand
The worth of a soul and the change that's wrought
By the touch of the Master's hand.

—Myra Brooks Welch - The Touch of the Master's Hand

The truth is we are all flawed and fallen people. Not one of us since Jesus has walked through life perfectly. The Lord is the One who gives us value and worth, if we allow Him to touch us.

Active involvement in missions allows God a chance to walk with us and show us things. The people we touch in His name can be impacted for all eternity, and in the process, indelibly, so are we. ❧

"When you need a marker whose ink will stand the test of time."

—Marks-A-Lot slogan

PASSAGE IV

WHAT'S MY MISSION?

Hearing What God Has to Say and Figuring
Out What You're Supposed to Do About It

*"Here is the test to find whether your mission on earth is finished:
If you're alive, it isn't."*

—Richard Bach

57

GO WHERE?

"Men wanted for hazardous journey. Small wages. Bitter cold.
Long months of complete darkness. Constant danger. Safe return
doubtful. Honor and recognition in case of success."

—Ernest Shackleton

Т HIS ACTUAL ADVERTISEMENT ran in the Times of
London on December 29, 1913, according to Hugh
Robert Mill in his 1923 biography The Life of Sir
Ernest Shackleton. It was an attempt to gather a crew for a ship
called the Endurance, which would soon be sailing on an expedition to Antarctica. Why? Because Ernie, their leader, was on
a mission to be the first man to cross the frozen continent by
way of the South Pole on foot with dogsleds. The boat would
drop the team off on one side of this five-and-a-half-million-
square-mile island, and they would walk across and get picked
up by the boat on the other side. It's about the same distance as
walking from New York to Los Angeles.

Simple, right?

Let's keep in mind just a few other things. The average tem-
peratures in Antarctica during the balmy summer months drop
to around negative thirty-five degrees Fahrenheit at night. The
wind chill factor makes it a bit worse: Antarctica has the most
ferocious winds recorded on this planet, which create blind-
ing snowstorms without warning. Nothing grows there except
maybe penguins, walruses, and sea lions, if you're near the water.

Antarctica is about as inhospitable a place as anywhere on earth. And before you even arrive in this unique climate, your wooden sailboat has to navigate the Drake Passage, a stretch of freezing water that shoots like an enormous fire hose between the tip of South America and northern Antarctica. Picture thousands of Amazon Rivers trying to squeeze together through a keyhole, constantly buffeted by gale-force winds, and you are an ant trying to navigate this upon your small twig of a boat.

Also bear in mind, back in 1914 they didn't have proper ship-to-shore radios, nuclear subs, or helicopters. You were on your own. If you got into trouble, that was your problem. The light generated by your emergency flare gun would be nothing more than a pretty fireworks show for your beleaguered crew. Even if you could call home, nobody would be dumb enough to come out there and get you.

Why would anyone sign up for an insane adventure like this? My answer is because people are people and, well, it's an adventure. God made some people adventurous. They want to go on adventures for various reasons.

"For the money, for the glory, and for the fun."
—Smokey and the Bandit

Your average person would expect Sir Ernest to have a hard time finding Englishmen to fill the bunks on his ship of the damned, certainly bound for a freezing death. Yet, his greatest difficulty was turning people away. His ad apparently generated over five thousand applications from men wanting to go with him.

Miraculously, nobody died on the voyage, and the story of Shackleton and the Endurance is one of the greatest tales of

hardship and survival in human history. It is well worth your time to read. That is, of course, if you're adventurous.

Were these men called by God to risk their lives? Maybe, but more than likely they just wanted to go. It was the earthly desire of their flesh to go on this adventure. They were built that way. The idea of possible earthly recognition turned them on as well. I know something about this desire for adventure, recognition, and attention. Don't you?

Some people will literally risk their lives for it. ❧

> *"I always knew how to draw a crowd."*
>
> **—Evel Knievel**

58

LEWIS AND CLARK

"Carpe diem, seize the day, boys, make your lives extraordinary."
—John Keating in Dead Poets Society

MY DAD ONCE REMARKED, as I was preparing to depart for another one of my missions out to the edge of the known world, "You know, son, we are so different. If you and I had lived in colonial America together, I would likely have run a bar or been a shop owner someplace like Philadelphia, and you would have surely hired on to risk your life with the Lewis and Clark Expedition."

Dad is not adventurous and has never understood my desire to wander far from home. His point was it is more safe, secure, predictable, and profitable to be engaged in commerce back in Philly. His protective, fatherly message to me: Perhaps I should stay home, get married, and settle down.

My rather defensive, young, egotistical, and "fleshly" response was, "Yeah, but Dad, how many history books did they write about the shopkeepers of colonial Pennsylvania?" I punctuated it with one of my favorite quotes, from Rear Admiral Grace Murray Brewster Hopper: "A ship in port is safe, but that is not what ships are for. Sail out to sea and do new things"

Dad always had a nice house and plenty of money to do whatever he wanted. I didn't always. There are indeed many downsides to going far afield and living the way I have. It's not for everyone, and should not be. There are plenty of missions right where you are, even inside your town or your own home.

You will have to gauge yourself, your experience, and the risk for yourself.

For better or for worse, I was deliberately built and prepared for international missions.

Here or far away: How were you built? Where is your mission? ✈

"For you created my inmost being; you knit me together in my mother's womb."

—Psalm 139:13

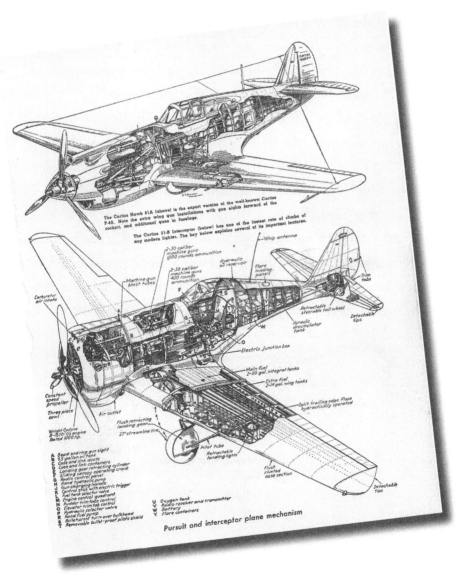

The Curtiss Hawk 81A (above) is the export version of the well-known Curtiss P-40. Note the extra wing gun installations with gun sights forward of the cockpit, and additional guns in fuselage.

The Curtiss 21-B Interceptor (below) has one of the fastest rate of climbs of any modern fighter. The key below explains several of its important features.

Pursuit and interceptor plane mechanism

59

THE KING'S SERVANT

EOPLE OFTEN ASK ME, "Why serve people in Peru or Cuba or anywhere else when there are people in need back home? What about the problems in the good ol' USA? You could share the love of Christ in the Rio Grande Valley of Texas with so many Latino immigrants. Or help the poor of the Appalachian Mountains. You could even minister to folks in the ghettos of New York, Detroit, or any other big city. Don't you want to help your own neighbors? Why go so far away from your home and people?"

My independent, free-spirited answer in the past was: because that's the "flavor" I choose. That's what I want and I do what I want. I'm in charge. I don't need God or anyone else.

However, as God's child and ambassador, and as a valued member of the Body of Christ, today my answer is: because that's the way the Lord made and prepared me. He built me that way. It wouldn't matter if I was a shopkeeper, teacher, or stay-at-home mom. We bloom where we're planted. Our mission has to do with how we were designed by our Creator.

"Some people are doctors, others fix bikes
Mothers bake cookies and boxers love fights
We all have talents that we're 'sposed to use
To win the attention of those still a'snooze"

—Stevie the Guide

I have deliberately surrendered control of my life to the Lord. I have asked my Father to confirm for me each earthly instinct or attraction to go in a particular direction toward a particular mission field in His service.

Let me repeat that. Today I no longer set out on my own purely self-serving missions, as I once did. Today all missions are in the service of my King, and I am but His humble servant and ambassador. I consult with Him first. Sure, I have a natural attraction to serve in specific parts of the world and in specific ways, but I seek His will. Being humble does not come to me naturally, but I work at it. I have allowed myself to be "in tune" with God as best as I know how.

Our flesh wants to go one way, but this may not be our Father's way. He will tell us what He wants us to do, but we may have to wait.

> Man in Black: "I'm afraid you'll just have to wait."
> Inigo Montoya: "I hate waiting."
> **—The Princess Bride**

God will reveal our mission in His own time. It will be revealed, if you are deliberately paying attention to God, His wishes, and His direction. ✎

> "But those who hope in the Lord will renew their strength. They will soar on wings like eagles; they will run and not grow weary, they will walk and not be faint."
> **—Isaiah 40:31**

60

SHARE THE LOVE

"To laugh often and much; to win the respect of intelligent people and the affection of children; to earn the appreciation of honest critics and endure the betrayal of false friends; to appreciate beauty; to find the best in others; to leave the world a bit better, whether by a healthy child, a garden patch or a redeemed social condition; to know even one life has breathed easier because you have lived. This is to have succeeded."

—Ralph Waldo Emerson

ACTIVELY SHARING LOVE the way Christ loved others can look all kinds of ways. Have you ever helped a stranger or volunteered anywhere?

Our first four years being involved in missions in Peru were a lot different than I ever imagined. We went down there to help manage a financially struggling orphanage, and we did a lot of business management and fund-raising. But this is also what the Lord did through our family:

We painted buildings. We restarted an abandoned pig farm. We played sports with kids. We guided medical teams to remote areas. We guided all kinds of teams and individuals. We helped build a couple of churches. We raised money for programs and projects. We organized art projects. We started Awana programs. We cut the grass. We washed clothes. We used chainsaws. We dug drainage ditches. We recruited experts in agriculture. We recruited lots of folks. We read kids to sleep. We worked on water treatment. We worked on waste manage-

ment. We bought supplies. We installed roofs. We did a lot of cleaning and mopping. We guided door-to-door evangelism teams. We mixed concrete. We drove the kids places in a van. We painted faces. We moved dirt and rocks in big trucks. We jarred honey and fruit preserves. We made jewelry. We recruited churches to get involved. We sang songs. We walked a long way. We built fires. We drew up blueprints and got building permits. We fought snakes. We ate crude local food to honor others. We drank lots of coca tea. We led people on tours. We tiled floors.

We did accounting. We hugged a lot of people. We visited numerous mud brick homes. We built people homes. We gave away Bibles. We worked in the garden. We cooked and served food. We installed irrigation. We fed the homeless and poor. We gave strangers a ride. We pulled abscessed teeth. We fitted people with eyeglasses. We hammered nails. We treated kids for lice. We cut hair. We played lots of soccer. We taught English and computer. We took people to the hospital. We cleaned wounds and stuck on Band-Aids.

We prayed constantly.

In short, we did anything people needed. While we were doing it, we talked about Jesus and what He has done for us. My favorite question from local people is "Why are you here helping us?" It can be said in many ways, but in short the answer is: God saved me through His Son, Jesus. These are the reasons why it has been good for my life, and I want to tell you why it's a good idea for you and everyone.

We witnessed to them. All the word witness means is that you have witnessed or seen the good things Jesus has done in your life and/or the life of others. Don't be afraid to share with people. Whether you discuss the Bible or not, you can share the importance of learning this book and knowing God better.

You can talk to them about Jesus and what He's meant to your life. 🐾

"In the same way, let your light shine before others, that they may see your good deeds and glorify your Father in heaven."

—Matthew 5:16

61

GOD SPOKE TO ME!

𝕴s GOD CALLING ME, or is it just my desire? It's a tightrope that can confuse which way to go if one is not really tuned into what God is trying to tell you.

"The call of God is the expression of God's nature, not ours. God providentially weaves the threads of His call through our lives and only we can distinguish them"

—Oswald Chambers

Get closer to the Lord through prayer and learning the Bible. Letting Him be the pilot, not the copilot, is a lifelong journey. Let the Lord use

you and work through you. Many bright thinkers are control freaks. I myself always want to grab the steering wheel and be in charge, but I will not usually be driving where God wants to go. Let Him drive, and be amazed where He takes you. You can't merely figure this one out intellectually—you have to feel it.

"Remember, a Jedi can feel the Force flowing through him."
—Ben Kenobi, Star Wars

They say you first have to die to yourself before you can live in Him. It's not easy for a guy like me to be a passenger in my own body and take the direction of another. Have faith! Don't over think. It works better that way. Didn't I just say we're dead already?

Where do you feel God driving you? ❧

"I no longer live, but Christ lives in me. The life I now live in the body, I live by faith in the Son of God, who loved me and gave himself for me."
—Galatians 2:20

"I believe God is managing affairs and that He doesn't need any advice from me. With God in charge, I believe everything will work out for the best in the end. So what is there to worry about?"
—Henry Ford

62

BE QUIET

"I had the right to remain silent ... but I didn't have the ability."

— Ron White

I F YOU ARE LIKE ME, your mind is thinking all the time about you, what you want, and what you think you should do next. I have learned about and tried to practice prayerful quiet times as best I am able; but it doesn't come naturally to me.

I am a busy doer who wants to run full throttle the minute my eyes pop open in the morning. I have found, however, if I am willing to settle in the first quiet moments of each day, I have a better chance of hearing God without me getting in the way.

"Goodbye. I love you. Settle down."

— dying words of my grandfather, H. George Schneider, to me

If you want to hear God speaking to you, you must allow Him the time and space to do so. Settle down.

Did you ever notice the words listen and silent have the same letters, just rearranged? Hmmm.

"The majority of us cannot hear anything but ourselves. And we cannot hear anything God says. But to be brought to a place where we can hear the call of God is to be profoundly changed."

—Oswald Chambers

There was a commercial on TV when I was a boy. An old man walked with a younger man down a busy, noisy street. The old gentleman turned and remarked to his friend, "Listen to the sound of that beautiful bird."

The younger man asked how he could hear the birdsong in the midst of the city commotion. The wise old guy stopped, pulled some change from his pocket, and tossed it on the ground with a faint clink, clink, clink as it hit the pavement. People passing by slowed and began looking around for the loose coins. The older man smiled and said, "People hear what they listen for."

You will not hear the Lord calling you to missions and directing your steps if you're not deliberately calmed down and tuned in. ✺

"Be still, and know that I am God."

—Psalm 46:10

63

HAT YAI

Zuzu: "Look, Daddy. Teacher says, every time a bell rings an angel gets his wings."
George: "That's right, that's right. Attaboy, Clarence!"

—It's a Wonderful Life

J WAS HOMELESS ONCE; at least it felt that way. It wasn't for very long, but I got a taste of it.

On the advice of a friend, I withdrew all the money I had, flew to Southeast Asia, and tried to get a job. Four months later, I was flat broke. Hindsight tells me it was a hasty decision.

The end of the line was Koh Samui Island, where the money dwindled. I tried not to think about it, but the day arrived when I had to bail. I had a plane ticket to Houston and a hundred-dollar bill at a friend's house in Singapore. All I had to do was get there.

Getting there involved a three-hour boat ride to the town of Surat Thani on the mainland, followed by a seven-hour bus ride at night to Hat Yai in central Thailand. There I would catch the twenty-two-hour express bus through Malaysia to Singapore. Simple. I had carefully calculated just how much it would cost. The trip from Koh Samui to Hat Yai went fine. I was hungry and sweaty on the converted school bus and very much looked forward to a nice breakfast in Hat Yai.

The bus arrived in Hat Yai around 9:00 a.m., and by 9:30 I located the express bus "terminal." It was not a building at all, but more like a walk-up window near the highway. A skinny man with little round glasses peered out at me curiously when I handed him the money for my ticket.

He smiled slightly, then frowned, shaking his head. "This not enough money!"

"What?" I protested feebly. "It has to be! They told me two weeks ago in Phuket what the price was! I need to get to Singapore. Please help me out here."

This guy was about as unsympathetic as Muhammad Ali would be in the twelfth round. The answer was no. The price had doubled. That was that.

I begged and groveled for mercy, but it didn't work. I had a small backpack with some clothes, a cheap camera, and a nice belt. Which one did he want? It was more like what did he not want? He even took my pack! I got to keep a single change of clothes in a plastic bag, but he finally gave me the bus ticket to Singapore. I was so relieved.

"What time does the bus leave this afternoon?"

"Not this afternoon. The day after tomorrow afternoon," he stated most indifferently.

"The day after tomorrow?!" I yelped. "I can't wait until then! What am I going to do until then?"

I launched into more protest, but the little man with round glasses wasn't having any. He slammed the window and drew the curtain. No further discussion. Sawadeekap (good day) to you.

I was in a state of shock and wandered with a blank stare. Dawning on me rapidly was the realization I was in about as strange a foreign city as one could possibly be in. I had no food, no money, no place to go for days, and then a long bus ride. Hat Yai is a hot, humid, bustling place with thousands of people going and doing. There was no open countryside nearby where one could lie down under a tree, pick an apple, and take a nap. It is an urban work machine.

My passage to Singapore was secure, but what was I going to do until then? It was ten in the morning, my bus didn't leave for the better part of three days, and then it was a twenty-two-hour trip. I didn't have even a dime for coffee, and I was already hungry and sweaty. For some folks, this may not seem like a big challenge, but for me it was quite a blow. I had hit an all-time low. My plans were not God's plans. I was a homeless person without a penny, and I could feel it instantly.

> *"You used to laugh about, everybody that was hangin' out*
> *Now you don't talk so loud.*
> *Now you don't seem so proud.*
> *About having to be scrounging for your next meal*
> *How does it feel?*
> *How does it feel?*
> *To be without a home?*
> *Like a complete unknown?*
> *Like a Rolling Stone."*
> **—Bob Dylan**

I wandered about Hat Yai, this strange town in Thailand that attracted hardly any tourists. I saw very few white faces to whom I could relate, and nobody was interested in my plight. I looked like one of those bag people with a two-day beard, wrinkled clothes, and a plastic sack containing all my worldly possessions. At one point I approached a guy from Europe and tried to explain my predicament. He grimaced and walked away as if I were a common, stinking bum. I felt like one.

It was one of life's most humiliating moments. I was as low as a cat's belly, and though I was not in the habit, I prayed to God for a miracle. I badly needed some help.

"If you believe, you will receive whatever you ask for in prayer."
—Matthew 21:22

The cars in the street whizzed by, and I stood on the curb staring blankly as the afternoon sun began to set. Catatonic in disbelief over my situation, I felt depressed desperation settling in. I was really tired, hungry, and exasperated. I didn't know what to do. I was trying to appraise which doorways and alleys might offer the least likelihood of a violent mugging while I slept.

I did not notice him approach, but all at once I turned to see a short, balding Chinese man smiling up at me. Our eyes met briefly, and I looked away, disinterested in whatever he was trying to sell. He stared at me with a happy Buddha face.

"Where you going?" he began. "What you doing?" Ignoring him most impolitely I turned further away, but he persisted. "Where you going?" He pressed again.

I flashed some attitude, hoping he'd go away. "I don't know what I'm doing or where I'm going!" I barked. "I don't have any money, I'm hungry, and I don't even have a place to sleep tonight! So whatever you're selling, I don't want any!"

I will never forget the next moments as long as I live. He gazed up at me with a warm smile, and I am sure I saw his eyes twinkle in the afternoon sun.

"Catholic church, right down the street," was all he said. He drew back his left hand over his right shoulder, as if winding up for a baseball pitch, then swept it outstretched toward his left. He pointed his stubby index finger toward a long, crowded boulevard. My eyes followed his finger, and for a few seconds, maybe the count of ten, I strained to see if what he said was true. Going to a church had never entered my mind in this Buddhist society. I could see no church from where I stood.

"Where?" I turned back in astonishment, but as if by magic, the happy Chinese man was gone. I whirled around and searched the street, my eyes darting up and down, but there was no trace of him. To this day it is one of the strangest feelings I have ever had, as if I had been visited by a divine messenger. His job completed, the "Angel of Hat Yai" disappeared on the breeze.

"For he will command his angels concerning you to guard you in all your ways."
—Psalm 91:11

I quickly pulled myself together. Lord knows I was a mess, but I was filled with hope. A church? A shot of adrenaline stood me up straight. Could this be real? A church? Well, I'll be jiggered. I scampered down the street, further down the street, and way on down the street, until sure enough, I could see a steeple. It was such a beacon! I approached the medium-sized cathedral complex with its school and other administrative buildings. Some adolescent Thai boys were playing basketball, and the only spectator sat on a courtside bench.

I walked up, put my plastic bag down, and appraised the man watching the game. There sat a balding, one-eyed priest with a black eye patch tied bandanna-style around his head. He wore flowing green-and-white robes with shiny pinkish rosary beads hanging from the waistband. I guesstimated his rhinoceroid form to be easily 350 pounds.

His head turned back and forth, back and forth as he watched the game. I was uncomfortable and didn't quite know what to say. I certainly didn't want to interrupt his enjoyment of the contest. I was a tired, grungy mess. So I simply sat down next to the father and watched the game, back and forth, back and forth. At one point, his single eye rolled around and peered in appraisal of me, but he said nothing.

The game ended. He congratulated the winners in Thai, shook some hands, then turned to me. "So what is your story?" he grumbled in a thick Italian accent.

I explained I needed shelter for a couple of nights. He quizzed me carefully and asked to see my passport. His watchful eye studied me for signs of deception. "Follow me," he said when I passed muster. Father Antonio took me to a clean, air-conditioned dormitory. (It was the beginning of school vacation, so there was no one living on campus.) He gave me a room, clean sheets, and a towel, and showed me the showers. I was dizzy with gratitude.

"Are you hungry? Of course you're hungry," he answered himself. Motioning me down a hallway, we entered a giant commercial kitchen. Pointing to the refrigerators he said, "Please help yourself to whatever you need, and don't make a mess. You are all by yourself here, so when you leave, lock this door behind you. I am departing now for my vacation and will not see you again."

I could not believe it. The place was mine. I was rescued! I thanked him profusely, as if I had been plucked from the open ocean by the Coast Guard.

Father Antonio laid that one eye on me very sternly for a long moment and pointed. "There is a chapel down at the end of that hallway. I suggest you say some prayers." Our eyes locked another moment as he appraised me, then he was gone. I never saw him again.

I steamed in the shower until I was wrinkled, made the bed with crisp white sheets, and ate till my heart was content. The refrigerator and pantry were stocked to the brim. I was clean, well fed, and safe. How did this happen?

I wandered down the quiet hallway to the chapel. The minute I entered the gentle light, I began crying softly, uncontrollably. It had been a long and absolutely overwhelming day. I needed so badly to talk to someone, and Jesus was there. I knelt down in front of the large cross with the Lord hanging there looking so tormented and bleeding. I prayed in earnest for maybe the first time in my life. It was so quiet in there.

Though it was but a brief experience, I now knew firsthand what it was like to have nothing and to have to go and ask a stranger for help. I thanked God for sending the angel who came to me in my time of trouble. I was so sorry for being rude and disrespectful to that nice Chinese man. He had led me with a wave of his hand to this kind priest, and to sanctuary. I had a new understanding of the word **sanctuary**.

> *"Do not forget to show hospitality to strangers, for by so doing some people have shown hospitality to angels without knowing it."*
>
> **—Hebrews 13:2**

I thanked God with all of my heart as I softly blubbered in the safety of this quiet place. It was so good to cry (some guys can't understand that). I thanked Him for the wonderful time I'd spent in Asia, for family, and for all of my many blessings. I was so lucky. I apologized for being selfish. I told Him I wished my time in Asia wasn't over, and how I had wanted to carry out my mission and find a job there. I talked with God a long while that night. It was wonderful.

Three days later I arrived in Singapore and with plans to soon catch the plane home to Texas. I answered a message from an oil exploration company asking me to come by their office. I didn't expect much; the oil business worldwide was in the tank in 1985. Companies weren't hiring, they were firing, but I went over there anyway. What did I have to lose?

It was a miracle! Instead of going to Texas broke, they sent me to China making more money than I had ever made in my life. I was reeling with amazement. It was the biggest mission ever, and I knew God was in it. His involvement was so obvious to me.

Hat Yai changed my life forever.

Have you ever had a moment when you felt the protection of angels? ❧

"Ask and it will be given to you; seek and you will find; knock and the door will be opened to you."

—Matthew 7:7

64

THEY JUST DON'T UNDERSTAND

YOUR RELATIONSHIP WITH CHRIST can never be clearly and completely understood by others. You were prepared by Him for a certain mission, and you will instinctively know it when you see it whether it makes sense to anyone else or not.

"It is useless to seek another person's opinion of it."
—Oswald Chambers

Remember that when your parents or friends are seeking an explanation as to why you have just bought an airline ticket to go serve in Indonesia because the Lord has called you there. Try to be comforting to them, but stick to what you alone are certain of.

It is your decision to answer what you believe is a genuine "calling from God." To participate in missions, whether short-term or long-term, local or international, is entirely yours and yours alone. There is nothing more important in this life.

Please bear in mind that if you are married and "one in Christ" with your spouse, it is an equally yoked, joint decision of your oneness. You must have a mutual recognition and desire to answer the call "as one." That's right, dude, you can't go unless your wife's on board.

So decide, and pursue the path you know you must take, leaving all other roads for someone else. ⚬

"I shall be telling this with a sigh
Somewhere ages and ages hence:
Two roads diverged in a wood, and I—
I took the one less traveled by,
And that has made all the difference."

—Robert Frost, "The Road Not Taken"

65

YOU MAY BE THE EXAMPLE

"Pull the trigger and ride the bullet."

—Roy H. Williams

IT'S HARD TO EXPLAIN your communication with the Almighty, especially if you have non-believing family members and friends. Do the best you can based on your understanding of them. Make a decision and carry on. By going ahead, you may just bring them around to see the Lord working through you. Part of your mission may very well be to set an example for the folks back home.

I can tell you one of our family members was adamantly opposed to my leaving a strong real estate practice and moving our kids to South America. "It's a bad business decision!" he protested. "You're endangering your family and depriving the girls of the American life to which they are entitled! Why are you doing this?"

He was genuinely concerned for our well-being and trying his best to protect us. I love him more than he knows for it. It was difficult to tell him, a very successful businessman, that the Lord God had called me and our family to serve orphans and the poor in Peru. He didn't like it, and he didn't understand it when we walked out the door and answered the call to serve. However, a year or so later, he came to visit and had a good look around.

There was never an obvious "aha!" moment, but his perspective naturally grew, and he asked many thoughtful questions.

We think he has become more understanding of our work and our calling as a result, and the change has been good to see. Because we stepped out in faith, even though we were afraid and under pressure, he and others have gained something new and refreshing. We are the only missionaries they know.

So try not to be afraid of the initial response from others. You need not share all the details about your communication with God. Your friends and family will see the Lord working through you, and they will be impacted one way or another.

"I wonder how far Moses would have gone if he'd taken a poll in Egypt? What would Jesus Christ have preached if he'd taken a poll in Israel? Where would the Reformation have gone if Martin Luther had taken a poll? It isn't polls or public opinion of the moment that counts. It is right and wrong and leadership."

—Harry S. Truman

If you're not getting resistance from somewhere, you're probably not doing enough. Ask yourself this: If you are called by God to a mission and you don't therefore, go, who will be their example? ❧

"Do not conform to the pattern of this world, but be transformed by the renewing of your mind."

—Romans 12:2

66

KABUL OR CABO?

"Only those who will risk going too far can possibly find out how far one can go."

—*T. S. Eliot*

I AM REMINDED OF A YOUNG GIRL named Sara, who was all of twenty-three years old when I met her in Texas some years ago. Sara attended a talk given by two American missionary women who had been held captive by the Taliban after the US invasion of Afghanistan. Sara had been "called" then and there. She was inspired to drop what she was doing, become a missionary, and go serve the Lord in Kabul, Afghanistan.

I was as supportive and encouraging as I could be to her, but privately, I thought she was crazy. Afghanistan? Taliban? The "rights" of women maybe included getting stoned by angry men if you lowered the veil on your burka to take a drink from a water fountain. The idea made my skin crawl! I thought of how I might feel if one of my daughters told me of this calling.

I mentioned this to a friend from church, Wally, who runs a print shop. "Kabul?!" he asked with a shocked tone and unbelieving stare. I thought his eyes were going to pop out of his head. "She said she's moving to Kabul? They just blew the crap out of that place! Those people hate us, especially women!" Wally's eyes darted blankly around in no particular direction for a few long, pensive moments. "Man, I think if I was her I'd be on my knees asking, 'Lord, is it Kabul, or Cabo?'"

I don't know whether or not Sara actually went to Afghanistan, but it was clear she felt called to the people and problems there. Clear passion was present. It didn't matter what anyone else thought. I hope God doesn't call my daughters to someplace like that, but you never know. Listen to the Lord, follow the passion He gives you, and therein lies the calling. ❧

That's What I'm Going to Do

For God is our Savior, He takes care of us
And what He wants us to do
Is frown at the evil, and smile at the good
Banish the evil, and take care of the good
So that's what I'm going to do!

—written by my daughter Ellie, age 5, published in
"Celebrating Poetry," 2002

67

ARMED TO THE TEETH

Prayer is a strong wall and fortress of the church; it is a goodly Christian weapon.

—Martin Luther

It cannot ever
be overstated.
These committed people
who regularly pray for you,
your family, and your mission
are the foundation
of everything you do.
They will actively intercede
with God through prayer
for all your hopes,
dreams, and needs.
Prayer warriors are the
best protection and often
the very best friends you can
have behind you when you are
preparing to answer the
Lord's call and head
out into the field,
far … far … away.
Or maybe you're just
going down the street.
I don't care how you do it
… but get some prayer covering.
Don't leave home without it. ❧

"The prayer of a righteous person is powerful and effective."

—James 5:16

68

CRAZY WILLY

"Do you think I've gone round the bend?"
"I'm afraid so. You're mad, bonkers, completely off your head. But
I'll tell you a secret. All the best people are."

—Lewis Carroll, Alice's Adventures in Wonderland

ILLY WAS FROM ENGLAND and lived between 1761 and 1834. People thought he was crazy. He read books about the worldwide voyages and adventures of the famous Captain James Cook, and he was set "afire" about the world around him.

Willy was a pastor and shoemaker, but his hobby and passion was global exploration. He studied different cultures, taught children about the world, drew maps, and even fashioned his own globe.

He felt a strong international calling from God and eventually wrote a book about global missions, An Enquiry, published in 1792. In it he made a case for initiating international missions efforts. This was clearly an absurd notion. Most people in England believed Willy should return to reality, stay home, and take care of real business. He kept pressing his fellow pastors to set up an international missionary agency, but they were always more interested in problems closer to England. At one meeting an older pastor reportedly snapped at him, "Young man, sit down! When God pleases to convert the heathen, he'll do it without consulting you or me."

However, Willy's adventurous spirit combined with his belief in God's call had started a movement that inspired people to share the love of Christ and help others in need around the world. Eventually, William Carey's passion led him to start the Baptist Missionary Society. The following year he set sail for India as their first missionary. During his time in India he:

- Formed a team of missionaries called the Serampore Trio.
- Helped translate the Bible into thirty-four Asian languages.
- Compiled dictionaries of Sanskrit, Marathi, Punjabi, and Telegu.
- Started Serampore College.
- Began churches and established nineteen mission stations.
- Formed one hundred rural schools encouraging the education of girls.
- Started the Horticultural Society of India.
- Served as a professor at Fort William College, Calcutta.
- Began the weekly publication "The Friend of India."
- Printed the first Indian newspaper.
- Introduced the concept of the savings bank to assist poor farmers.
- Fought against the burning of widows, which led a ban on the custom in 1829.

I could go on if space permitted, but you get the idea. His accomplishments are too numerous to list here. On top of all that, "Crazy Willy" inspired tens of thousands to serve the poor and share the gospel worldwide. He spent forty-one years doing missionary service and never returned to England.

Some people still thought William Cary was crazy, but he didn't care. He was not seeking their opinions. 🕊

"Expect great things from God; attempt great things for God."

—William Carey

69

HEADQUARTERS

"Missions is not the 'ministry of choice' for a few hyperactive Christians in the church. Missions is the purpose of the church."

—author unknown

THE PRIMARY ANCHOR and source of support for your mission should always be your home church. Note that they may or may not be a source of financial support for your mission. Churches and missions committees are just groups of people with various priorities. Your mission may or may not be one of them, but stay close, and don't leave home without a solid church relationship.

Let the church know immediately when you feel the Lord is calling you to missions, either short- or long-term. Talk it over with them regularly, open lines of communication, and get a game plan. This will be invaluable to you before, during, and after your time in the field.

Hey, James Bond has a home office, MI6, with authorities he answers to. Same deal ... sort of.

Pay attention to your church leaders and partners. If they offer classes or books, get in there! Courses like Perspectives and Panorama will raise your awareness exponentially, whether you're planning to spend a week or the rest of your life in the mission field. These can be great resources for equipping you with information you may not have. Remember, when you first get excited about missions, your natural inclination is to want to "therefore, go." But let seasoned veterans help guide and prepare you for what you're doing.

There are apparently many missions sending agencies in the US for long-term missionaries. We have been a part of the Commission to Every Nation (CTEN) family in Kerrville, Texas, and have loved every minute. Sometimes missionaries just work with their church, and this can be great. However, churches are often not very well equipped to handle the needs of their people once they're out in the field. Things like printing and mailing your newsletter, orientation, pastoral care visits, IRS year-end, nonprofit reporting, and receipts to donors can be a lot of work for a church office to handle.

The missions agency basically becomes your nonprofit partner in conjunction with your church. In our case, we paid 10 percent of every dollar we raised to CTEN for the services mentioned above. It was a small price to pay for all they've done for us. We could not have taken our family on a mission to Peru for several years without them.

Just like companies, missions agencies have various ways of doing business. Take your time and talk to several of them. I think you'll be glad you did! ❧

"Have confidence in your leaders and submit to their authority,
because they keep watch over you as those who must give an
account."

—Hebrews 13:17

Whatever you can do, or dream you can . . . begin it. Boldness has genius, power and magic in it.

Goethe

70

WRITE A NEWSLETTER

"Before you can inspire with emotion, you must be swamped with it yourself. Before you can move their tears your own must flow. To convince them, you must yourself believe."
—Winston Churchill

IT IS SUCH AN EASY THING to do, but so many people won't do it: You must tell the world how you truly feel.

It's often pride that keeps you from sending out a letter saying you are a missionary and you want money from the public. Some would rather die. I know about this.

As I said earlier: Got pride? Get rid of it!

The Bible talks about this over, and over, and over. Pride will keep you from fulfilling your mission and get you into all kinds of troubles. Put pride aside, and you will find you're more comfortable opening up about your calling.

Share your true heart with people, the mission God has laid before you, and you will find supporters eagerly rising up to come alongside.

"People want to be part of something larger than themselves. They want to be part of something they're really proud of, that they'll fight for, sacrifice for, that they trust."
—Howard Schultz, CEO of Starbucks

Newsletters need to say just a few things in a clear way. If you write too much, you will lose or confuse people. Your newsletter should briefly include:

- Who you are
- With whom you are affiliated (church, mission agency, winging it on your own)
- Endorsements from people who believe in you (pastor, other supporters, etc.)
- Where you're going
- What you're doing
- Why it's important
- Why you need prayers and financial support
- How much money you need and where to send it
- Your photo and perhaps photos of where you're going

If at all possible, the newsletter should be in color, and most important, it should communicate that your vision is from God. He is calling you, and they need to know that.

Keeping your team connected with the mission is vital. If your mission is short-term, write a full report on the mission when you return home, and even deliver that report personally to your supporters with photos and video. If you do this well, your chances of gaining support for the next mission will rise dramatically. A long-term mission will require regular communication, reporting and keeping your support team connected all the time.

Send out your letter to everyone you can think of, and give it to anyone with whom you come into contact daily. You will be amazed at what happens. People want to be part of your mission. You are not out begging for money; you are offering them the chance to partner with something great for the Lord's

Kingdom. They won't have a chance to be part of this mission if you don't give the opportunity. Tell them through your letter. ❧

"Go tell it on the mountain, over the hills and everywhere."

—John W. Work Jr.

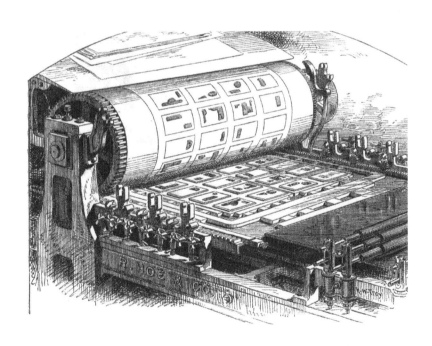

71

FARMER RICK

"Listen to advice and accept discipline, and at the end you will be counted among the wise."

—Proverbs 19:20

Y GRANDFATHER WAS ABSOLUTELY SHATTERED in 1929. By all accounts, Granddaddy Eddie was a broken man physically, emotionally, and economically.

Early in the year he was injured so badly that he could not continue with his chosen profession. His childhood hopes and dreams of making it to the top of the heap and being the best of the best were gone. He was let go from his job. There was no insurance. Family members say that when he finally came to terms with this harsh reality and understood it was all over, he broke down and cried like a baby to his young wife, my grandmother.

Fortunately, he had been investing the family money wisely, so they had plenty of financial cushion to weather the painful, uncertain transition. This offered many choices for a new start. Unfortunately, the stock market crashed in October of that year and wiped them out completely. Along with millions of other Americans, the family went to bed one night sleeping soundly on the certainty of a fat bank account, and woke up the next morning to the horror of economic catastrophe. For many days they couldn't believe it and tried to find the hard-earned greenbacks that no longer existed. My grandparents were flat broke. Again, they say, my big, strapping grandfather broke down and cried to his young, pregnant wife.

The next month, they had their first baby, and again Granddaddy cried. My dad was born on November 7, 1929. Though happy, the family had another mouth to feed. What was he going to do now?

"Oh, somewhere in this favored land the sun is shining bright,
The band is playing somewhere, and somewhere hearts are light;
And somewhere men are laughing, and little children shout;
But there is no joy in Mudville—mighty Casey has struck out."

—Ernest Lawrence Thayer, "Casey at the Bat"

* * *

We cleaned out my grandmother's dusty attic when she died at age 89. It was then, shuffling through an ancient trunk full of papers, that we learned my grandfather had an older friend, clearly his mentor, who was a working farmer. He encouraged Granddaddy to stop looking back and to become a farmer too.

Granddaddy didn't want to hear this at first. It wasn't the job he had hoped for, but it was a job that would at least keep him close to the profession he so loved. Farmer Rick spoke gently but firmly into Granddaddy's life. He encouraged him to "shake it off, grit his teeth, and bow his neck." He told him to reach inside himself, to lean on his many other strengths, to help others shine, and to look for the brightness of tomorrow. Evidently, Granddaddy listened.

Farmer Rick was a wise man. Not only did he help Granddaddy get started farming, but he constantly coached and encouraged him each growing season about how to choose the correct seeds, in what soil to plant them, and the proper amount of water, warmth, and specific nutrients the crop needed to grow tall and vibrant. "Rickey" put Granddaddy under his wing, and they became lifelong friends.

It took some time for the pain of loss to wear off for Granddaddy, but it wasn't long before he was thriving as a farmer and growing healthy crops all over the nation. He put the past behind him and stopped dwelling on the things that might have been. I think he was glad he did. Farmer Rick was not around all the time, but he sent many letters to teach and propel my granddaddy's farming career over the years. The following is one of the earliest notes, from 1932:

> *Dear Eddie,*
>
> *Among corn growing farmers there comes a time every season when the corn receives its last cultivation. The crop is then said to be "laid by."*
>
> *That does not mean that the crop is a good crop, that it does not need more rain, enough sunshine, freedom from germ pests, or early frost. It simple means that insofar as the farmer has been able to help the corn, he has done his job. That is what "laying by" means.*
>
> *Except for emergency treatment, your team is just about "laid by," as far as I am concerned. I think you have a good club. It may not win the pennant, and yet I think there is a good chance of your doing that very thing. Talk pennant to your men. Keep championship ideas in their heads. You must remember that Hannibal and Napoleon, and all the great generals in their camps kept foremost before their men constantly the rewards of victories. Now baseball championships have some spoils connected with winning, and it is a good thing to have the players keep these spoils in mind.*

You are the manager of your club because you have shown some marks of leadership, chief among which I choose to think may be the quality of persistent effort. If you never give up, sooner or later you will have a team that never gives up. I would be disappointed if anything I say here would cause you to "press" too much, or to make your men too tense. It is entirely possible for a manager to have his men keyed up to too high a pitch. They become over-tense, and try too hard. I do not know that it could happen in your case, but it has happened in the years gone by in my own case. Nevertheless, I urge you not to give up the chase for the pennant this very year, for I think you have a capable club....

Don't fail to write me, or call me in case of emergency, at any time. My plans can be changed very quickly, and I will be ready to do anything possible to help you upon your call."

Sincerely yours, Branch Rickey

My granddaddy, Eddie Dyer, spent most of his career dreaming about playing big league baseball. He never stopped hurting over injuring his arm, losing his job as a pitcher, and the fame and fortune that might have been. However, he got over it with the help of a wise friend and took a much lesser position without much prospect for glory. Relatively speaking, few people knew of him.

Granddaddy was going to quit managing minor league baseball farm teams in 1945 when his buddy Branch Rickey helped him get his dream shot for all the years of hard, unglamorous "farm" work. Granddaddy became the rookie manager of the Saint Louis Cardinals in 1946, and that year the Cards went all the way. After they won the 1946 World Series, it seemed like everyone knew Grandaddy's name.

Do you have a mentor? Is there anyone older and wiser trying to speak into your life? They may say something you don't want to hear, but I encourage you to listen. It could pay off in ways you never dreamed. 🏃

"I realized how much our relationship had deepened after I left baseball. It was that later relationship that made me feel almost as if I had lost my own father. Branch Rickey, especially after I was no longer in the sports spotlight, treated me like a son."

—Jackie Robinson

EDDIE DYER

For 'The Ole Lefthander'

Baseball World to Pay Dyer Tribute Tonight

By MORRIS FRANK
Eddie Dyer, the Houston boy who
was lent to the National league to
rescue that loop's prestige in the
baseball world, officially comes back
home Thursday night.
The 46-year-old Eddie, who has

testimonial dinners ever thrown
anywhere.
It will be Houston's tribute to its
beloved lefthander and it will be
more than that.
It will be the tribute of the en

St. Louis National Baseball Club

GROUNDS
Sportsmans Park
GRAND BLVD & DODIER ST.

OFFICES
3623 DODIER ST.

Cardinals

St. Louis, Mo.   July 23, 1932.

Mr. Edwin C. Dyer, Manager
Springfield Base Ball Club,
Springfield, Missouri.

Dear Eddie:

Among corn growing farmers there comes a time every season when the corn receives its last cultivation. The crop is then said to be "laid by".

That does not mean that the crop is a good crop, that it does not need more rain, enough sunshine, freedom from germ pests, or early frost. It simply means that insofar as a farmer has been able to help the corn, he has done his job. That is what **"Layin by"** means.

Except for emergency treatment, your team is just about "laid by", as far as I am concerned. I think you have a good club. It may not win the pennant, and yet I think there is a good chance of your doing that very thing. Talk pennant to your men. Keep championship ideas in their heads. You must remember that Hannibal and Napoleon, and all great generals in their camps kept foremost before their men constantly the rewards of victories. Now baseball championships have some spoils connected with winning, and it is a good thing to have the players keep these spoils in mind.

You are the manager of your club because you have shown some marks of leadership, chief among which I choose to think may be the quality of persistent effort. If you never give up, sooner or later you will have a team that never gives up. I would be disappointed if anything I say here would cause you to 'press' too much, or to make your men too tense. It is entirely possible for a manager to have his men keyed up to too high a pitch. They become over-tense, and try too hard. I do not know that it could happen in your case, but it has happened in the years gone by in my own case. Nevertheless, I urge you not to give up the chase for the pennant this very year, for I think you have a capable club.

I shall be ready to come to you at any time that I can be of service, but my present itinerary is as follows:
    In care of the ST. LOUIS OFFICE up to and including Monday, Aug. 1.
    KEOKUK, IOWA- in care of Iowa Hotel ....Tuesday, Aug. 2.
    COLUMBUS, OHIO   "   Deschler Hotel......... Wednesday, Aug. 3.
    HARRISBURG, PA   "   Columbus Hotel .... Thursday Aug. 4
                         (Elmira Club)

Mr. Edwin C.Dyer,Manager,
#2 July 23, 1932
_____

    New York,N.Y.   In care of Alamac Hotel   Friday,Aug.5
    "   "   "   "   Saturday,Aug.6
    "   "   "   "   Sunday,Aug.7

    Greensboro,N.C.   "   O'Henry Hotel   Monday, Aug.8
    "   "   "   Tuesday, Aug.9
    Elmira, N.Y.   " Mark Twain "   Thursday, Aug.11

    St.Louis Office ....   Friday, Aug.12

Don't fail to wire me, or call me in case of emergency, at any
time. My plans can be changed very quickly, and I will be ready
to do anything possible to help you upon your call.

               Sincerely yours,

                       Branch Rickey
                       Branch Rickey
                       Vice President.

BR:MM

72

GET YOUR 20

"The man who thinks he can and the man who thinks he can't are both right. Which one are you?"

—Henry Ford

S O, HOW DO WE PROMOTE our mission?

I once worked for a real estate broker who was a good teacher. He said my primary job was to let the general public know I helped people buy and sell real estate. I was to let at least twenty new people know every day. How would I do this? The very best way, he said, was to hand out flyers or at least my business card directly to another person every day. This broker said that if you can put your information into someone's hand, perhaps talk with them and shake their hand, your odds will go up dramatically in making a sale. He was right.

At the end of every day he would say, "I've got my 20! Do you have yours?" If you admitted to this guy that, well, no, you had not handed out twenty business cards or flyers that day, he took no excuses: "Walmart is open till nine p.m. Go stand in front of the door and hand out cards until you've got your twenty. Then you can go home and have dinner. If you don't feel like doing it, then you don't want to succeed bad enough here. Maybe it's time you started looking for a lesser brokerage to work for." He liked to end with: "The waste management and food service industries could use a guy like you!"

You gotta want your mission and be willing to share it with everyone you meet. You are excited! And understand that "casting your vision" and promoting your mission is a big part of the mission. If a guy gives you a dollar or prays for you, he has joined your mission team! He now has a vested interest in seeing what the Lord will do through you—and through him or her—on this mission.

Cheap flyers are easy to make. Include photos of you and your mission field, a little information, how to contact you, and how to make out the check. Most churches and missions sending agencies allow checks to be written to them on your behalf so that the donor can get a tax write-off.

You have to believe in God's mission more than you care about your own comfort zone. By stepping out and sharing with the family of Christ, your family, you will inspire and encourage them. Oh, and by the way, who is your family? What do they look like? It is the people around you, not just your biological family and friends.

Your family in Christ may work at a gas station, restaurant, or barber shop. They may look like the policeman who stops you or the person who helps you with your taxes. The Body of Christ is anyone, and they are potentially everywhere. Start looking for reasons to bring up your mission in conversations with others.

God will open up a new world for you, and you will be amazed at who steps up to take the honor of being on your mission support team. Be obedient to the call and cast your vision. Abundant resources will appear from places you never imagined! ❧

When He had finished speaking, He said to Simon, "Put out into deep water, and let down the nets for a catch."

Simon answered, "Master, we've worked hard all night and haven't caught anything. But because you say so, I will let down the nets."
And when they had done so, they caught such a large number of fish that their nets began to break.

—Luke 5:4-6

73

THE CHANGING FACE OF MISSIONS

"You never get bored with God in action."

—Loren Cunningham

I TELL PEOPLE I DO MISSIONARY work, and sometimes they envision a guy with a crucifix, black robes, and a little whip he beats himself with when his mind momentarily strays from the Lord. The ideas and misconceptions people have about missionaries can be seen in movies like *The Mission*, with Robert De Niro and Jeremy Irons. Over the years, many missionaries were ordained Catholic priests, Franciscan monks, and later, Protestant pastors.

Today there is a freedom of missionary service which has no limits. Any believer can get involved. I promise you. Whatever you can imagine to draw people's attention to the Lord and share His message or to care for His people in His name—I'm here to tell you it is possible.

The face of missionary service is changing. There are people doing all kinds of wild and creative stuff out there. These men and women are usually still very connected to their home churches, but they are not necessarily told what to do as in the past. They get to choose how to serve God in the mission field, and boy, do they choose some amazing, creative ways to serve the Lord and realize their dreams!

"Somewhere, over the rainbow, skies are blue.
And the dreams, that you dare to dream,
Really do come true."

—E. Y. Harburg and Harold Arlen

For example:

- I know guys who guide hikes and hold Christian leadership training seminars along the way, offering treks in Africa, Ireland, and Peru.
- There are missionaries who minister to surfers in beach communities all over the world, and some follow the international surfing tournament circuit.
- There are motocross missionaries who guide hair-raising bike tours in the rural Andes and Amazon to raise funds for Christian orphanage and school projects.
- Music missions.
- Mechanics missions.
- Horseback missions.
- There are guys who do nothing but drill water wells.
- I know missionaries who teach Zapotec Indian women in Mexico how to generate income by making quilts, jewelry, and handicrafts.
- One guy developed a coffee processing and packaging plant in Cambodia to sustain a hospital ministry.
- There are missionaries right now developing a gold mining operation in Suriname to sustain a tribe of remote indigenous people.
- One missionary friend and his family are leaving for England and France to use his architectural skills for church and ministry construction.

- A woman we know develops beer coasters and other pub promotions to raise awareness about slave trafficking.
- There are missionaries who develop Web pages and print materials.
- A friend of ours shoots video worldwide for other missionaries trying to tell their stories and cast their visions to the Body of Christ.
- Some missionaries do accounting and teach computer skills.
- We helped restart an abandoned hog farm and opened a general store and restaurant to sustain a Christian orphanage.
- We know biker missionaries who ride up to the annual motorcycle rally in Sturgis, South Dakota, to minister to the hardest gangs.
- Others do traditional things like preaching, vacation Bible school, and door-to-door evangelism in every country on earth.
- Missionary pilots fly teams to remote destinations all over the world.
- We've heard of a missionary sailor in Fiji who takes needy people where they need to go in the island archipelago, sharing the gospel along the way.
- There are prison missions of all kinds. (You will see one of mine in this book.)
- One missionary I know chases disasters wherever they happen: hurricanes, tidal waves, earthquakes, you name it.
- Missionaries are in every facet of the medical/dental field.
- Teachers of every variety.

No matter what skills, gifts, or passions you have, you can use them to share the love of Christ and build His Kingdom. Christian missionaries of today are often not seminary graduates. They are ordinary folks who love the Lord and have a desire to do whatever they can to serve Him and their fellow man. I call them "seed planters."

Young people should check out Youth With a Mission (YWAM). They train and send young folks all over the planet to do every mission there is.

I do understand it can be an awkward transition in your thinking. The thought of missionary service was new for me, too. It wasn't a part of my upbringing. I thought you had to have a degree or something.

My Catholic family was quick to point out I wasn't even "clergy," just a mere layman. What did I know about missionary work? Well, not much, and I was afraid of it for a long time. I have to admit it took me years to actually step up and get involved, first with short-term missions, and eventually working long-term in Peru and Cuba. No telling where it will lead us next!

Our first steps out into the mission field of Peru were full of surprises. We hit some bumps in the road, and I didn't always know what to do. I quickly recognized that I knew more about the business world, than how to use the Bible as my guide. But by going, we are learning. It has truly been an education we could never have gotten from a textbook. We had to "therefore, go" to get the awareness and new perspective we have now. As I'm fond of saying, "In the going you will develop the knowing."

We certainly don't know it all on this lifelong journey; however, by going to the mission field, our knowledge of missions took a quantum leap. For all the trouble and challenges, I am

so very glad I answered the Lord's call and decided to therefore, go. It has changed my life for the better, forever, in so many ways.

It can change yours, too. Start on a small mission. It doesn't matter if it's around your town or around the world. Step out there and declare publicly who you are. It will open doors you never imagined. ❧

"Take the first step in faith. You don't have to see the whole staircase, just take the first step."

—Martin Luther King Jr.

PASSAGE V
EXCUSES, EXCUSES

Turning Resistance into Motivation

*"You can either stand there on the beach and holler at
the waves, or you can wax down your surfboard, get
out there, and learn to ride."*

—Banzai Pipeline surfer, North Shore, Oahu

74

THE MISSIONS MAVERICK

"We're going ballistic, Mav, go get 'em."
—Goose in Top Gun

LIKE FOR PEOPLE TO THINK I'm a well-organized expedition guide and world-class explorer. The truth is I am more of a runaway than any of those things. I was always seeking ways to escape the crowd, get off the tour, and live by my own rules. There were times I had to be forced back in line or back to class. When faced with God and the mission He had for me, I did the biblical thing. I ran away like Jonah. For years I didn't even want to listen. I wouldn't row the boat, fly the plane, or even accept the gift. I have been in the belly of the fish. I was afraid, and maybe a little crazy. I'm still a little of both.

Though I'd rather liken myself to a sleek African animal like a leopard or kudu, the first animal that comes to mind for me is a stray cow. In Texas we have a name for this type of hardheaded creature: maverick. A maverick is:

- An unbranded range animal, especially a calf that has become separated from its mother; traditionally considered the property of the first person who brands it. (The term maverick is attributed to Texas lawyer Samuel Augustus Maverick (1803-1870), a cattleman who left the calves in his herd unbranded.)

- One who refuses to abide by the dictates of or resists adherence to a group. Does not follow the crowd.
- One who creates or uses unconventional and/or controversial ideas or practices.
- Creators who make business an adventure.
- Hard to control, may not play well with others.
- One who is different by choice.
- An electro-optically guided US air-to-ground tactical missile for destroying tanks and other hardened targets at ranges of up to fifteen miles.
- The guy in your office who thinks he's Tom Cruise in Top Gun. He's already seen the movie over five hundred times. He likes to use the word wingman and enjoys doing flybys over your air control tower.
- Being independent in thought and action or exhibiting such independence.

For better or worse, I have been a maverick. I have often run from the crowd, from authority, and from God. I have hide-outs around the planet in places most people have never even heard of. I've done my own thing and gone my own way, not wishing to be "controlled" by anyone or anything. I didn't want to listen to God or go to church.

"But Jonah ran away from the Lord and headed for Tarshish. He went down to Joppa, where he found a ship bound for that port. After paying the fare, he went aboard and sailed for Tarshish to flee from the Lord."

—Jonah 1:3

Who were these churchgoing Christian "believers," anyway? Many of them had phony-looking grins on their faces, as if they knew something I didn't. What did they want, and why were they so interested in talking to me? If I visited their church just because I was curious, they would want me to fill out a card with my contact info so they could get me "on the grid" and track me. Then they would call me repeatedly and try to get me to come to classes, orientations, Bible studies, parties, and "life groups"! This used to give me the willies.

Morpheus: "They're coming for you, Neo. And I'm not sure what they're going to do."
Neo: "What ... do they want with me?!"
Morpheus: "I'm not sure. But if you don't want to find out, you better get out of there."

—The Matrix

I ran all around the world, which led me to many adventures and exciting experiences. At times it also left me feeling disconnected, alone, and without strong direction.

Once upon a time I ran from God, church, and deep personal relationships, considering them a burden. Later I longed for the love of one good woman and being surrounded by a loving family. I have been richly blessed, since my surrender, with a dedicated "Proverbs woman" and two beautiful daughters for whom I have the deepest devotion. I get to serve in several kinds of missions, and I never grow bored with my work. I get to engage with some of the most wonderful people in the Body of Christ, and we serve in exotic places.

I strongly believe none of this would have happened if I were not the son of a God who loved and actively pursued me. I was His unbranded stray calf, and I had a lot of energy to burn off. Had He not doggedly chased after me and initiated contact again and again, I would have kept running until I dropped, and I would be in a completely different place right now.

"All of us know something about running away from God. We've been there. Wanting to live out our own lives; wanting to do our own thing; wanting to call our own shots. Therefore, we just get up and run... But the beautiful thing about God the Father is that He does not just let us run away and go our own way. He runs after us. That's the Hound of Heaven. And He runs after us as long as we continue to run.... But instead of a hound that consumes us, we find that God running after us was a loving heavenly Father. And He gives to us all of those things we were seeking, and hoping to find in our running away. Then we are to live out the rest of our lives, not running from God, but running with and in God, and we are to live out the rest of our lives in the posture of receiving."

—Dr. Ed Young

Are you a maverick too? Are you running from the Lord or from actively being involved in His service? Are you hiding "in the bushes" at the back of your church, or worse, not going at all, hoping no one will notice you? Maybe it's time for you to stop, turn, and see who's really chasing you. At least in my case, surrendering and being captured is not a one-time experience. The very fabric of my maverick nature is to run, evade arrest, and avoid capture. Does this sound familiar to you?

My hope is that by sharing my crazy experiences, more folks will get involved in missions. Stop looking for reasons not to serve the Lord, and listen to Him. Find your role in this play, your rightful place on this stage. It has made my life extraordinary.

I hope you don't miss it. ❧

75

THE POVERTY MENTALITY

"If it's the Lord's will, it's the Lord's bill."

—Rudy Johnson, Tambo de Gozo Missionary Retreat Center, Peru

I CAN'T AFFORD A TRIP like that!

The number one reason many people decide not to go on a short-term mission is not because they aren't interested or inspired. It's not because they don't feel called to go. I think they often really do feel the Lord's "tug," but the reason they decline and don't answer this calling is more about the cash. They think it is just too expensive.

You may have heard about a short-term mission in your church. Maybe they announced it in the sanctuary, or maybe they had a missions fair with lots of booths and ethnic food. Somebody in your Sunday school class or Bible study group may have encouraged you to go. In fact, you may have had an interest and wanted to go, but your bubble burst when you found out how much it would cost.

I remember when Sheri and I heard about a short-term mission to Peru at our church. I was so excited! I had been to Peru and very much wanted the girls to experience missions there. I started dreaming, and then I stopped. Trip cost per person: $1,600. Ouch! There was no way. I could not afford to take my family on this mission. It was too expensive.

My problem at that moment was the same problem I have had about many things in "my" life and missionary work: It was all about me. I was me-focused, and that's why my family and I were not going on this mission to Peru. "I" could not afford for us to get involved. Period. I really did not have the $6,000+ for us to blow on a trip. At the time, it was what my brother-in-law, Peter, calls a GBSD (grandiose bull$%!# dream). Just for the record, I don't call it that, but Peter does. Just sayin'.

So I finally got over my pride and sent out a letter, and my rich family, the Body of Christ, responded.

(See the chapters on prayer, newsletters, and by all means, "Get Your 20.")

If you are ever to be involved in Christian missions, there are so many reasons you need to stop thinking in terms of yourself. If you are not blessed with loads of financial resources, this does not in any way mean you cannot participate. It actually means you have a larger role to play.

When you pass by that missions booth or get encouraged by a church member to go on a mission, it is not the same as a vacation. You are not passing by a travel agency or getting invited to go on a leisure trip, even though it may sound fun and exciting. In the truest sense, you are being asked to run God's errand.

Until you can quit thinking about "me" and wrap your heart and mind around the magnitude of who you really are, what you are being asked to do, and who it's for, it will be hard for you to tap into that awesome power when you are trying to get involved and find provision.

When I just looked at "little old me," there was no way I could take my family on this mission; it wasn't going to happen. Yet, when I began to buy into the notion that I was one of many actors being invited to play a role on God's grand stage in His big production, my perspective changed. Yours will too. ❧

Jake: *"Ma'am, would it make you feel any better if you knew that what we're asking Matt here to do is a holy thing?"*
Elwood: *"You see, Mrs. Murphy, we're on a mission from God."*

—The Blues Brothers

76

A DRUNKEN THIEF

"You're gonna have to serve somebody
Well, it may be the devil or it may be the Lord
But you're gonna have to serve somebody"

—Bob Dylan

EORGE HAD A BAD HABIT of stealing money from his dad, and more than once, he sneaked out of a hotel without paying for the room. He frequented bars, drank a lot, and enjoyed being the life of the party. He also liked to make fun of people, especially Christians. George was not a guy you would peg as having great spiritual faith or even good moral character. He was a bit of a loser and was eventually caught by the police and ended up in jail.

One day he went to a Bible study with a friend, just to make fun of the Christians. To his surprise, George liked studying the Bible, and he liked being around people who knew and loved the Lord. He started going to church all the time. Pretty soon, his boozing buddies didn't want to be around him anymore; he just wasn't the same old guy.

The day George told his father he wanted to be a missionary, Pop hit the roof! How could George ever get a high-paying job if he was stuck on this idiotic notion? He told his son he was cutting off the money for school, but George knew what the Lord was calling him to do. He didn't know how to pay his tuition, so he did something way out of his comfort zone: George knelt and prayed for God's provision. An hour later, the answer came. A professor knocked on the door of his dorm room and offered George a paid tutoring job! He was amazed, and this was the beginning of his dependence on God.

George was called to be a missionary serving children in London. He walked the streets and saw hungry orphans everywhere, so he started an orphanage. Resources were scarce, but he prayed for a building, people to manage it, furniture, and money for food and clothing. God answered his prayers, and the needs were met each day, sometimes at the last minute.

He once prayed with three hundred children in the orphanage dining room, thanking God for breakfast when there was not a scrap of food in the house. A few minutes later, a baker showed up with some bread, and a milkman arrived to say his cart had broken down right by the front door. The milk would spoil if he didn't give it to the kids. George Müller was faithful, and God provided, every time.

Thousands of children lived in that orphanage over the years. When each became old enough to leave, George would pray with him and put a Bible in his right hand and a coin in his left. He explained to the young person that if he held onto what was in his right hand, God would always make sure there was something in his left hand as well.

You can see the story of George Müller's life in a video called Obstacle to Comfort. He was an ordinary, sinful guy who partnered with God to accomplish the extraordinary in missions.

Are you ordinary too? What do you suppose God is hoping to accomplish through you? 🌺

"The beginning of anxiety is the end of faith, and the beginning of true faith is the end of anxiety."
—George Müller, 1805-1898

77

CLOSET CASE?

$\mathfrak{I}$F YOU ARE AS TRULY INVESTED in this Christian walk as you say you are in private, then will you say so publicly?

Do you realize that sharing about a mission and raising support is a golden opportunity? It's part of the mission. Letting people know your faith helps build the Kingdom in your community as well as around the world. The mission is here and now, not there and then.

Quick review:

- You feel called to go on a mission.
- You might not personally have the money to go.
- Your faith is real.
- You are a member of the family of Christ.
- You trust God's direction and provision for His missions.
- You are willing to tell your "family" what God is doing in your life and what you need to accomplish this.

That last one is the kicker, isn't it? You really have to "come out of the closet," don't you?

Hoover: "Kent is a legacy, Otter. His brother was a '59, Fred Dorfman."
Kent: "He said legacies get asked to pledge automatically."
Otter: "Oh, well usually, unless the pledge in question turns out to be a real closet case."
Otter and Boon: "Like Fred."

*—**Animal House***

Are you a "closet case" for the Lord?

Do you really believe God and His missions are real? Do you believe you are His worthy family member? Are you proud to say so? Are you therefore willing to communicate openly with God's family about the mission He is calling you to, and for which you may need provision?

If not, forget about the mission trip. Take a vacation. Even if you have the money, you don't get it. Come back when you do.

If so, get excited! You now have a new, cool, and really good reason to step out and share your faith with people.

You are on a mission the second you get excited about one. It's not when you leave home and the plane takes off; it's right now! You are a missionary on a mission. The first steps are casting the vision and building your team. You're already underway.

Get going. Create materials, and tell everyone!

Carry the "message to Garcia." Go "tell it on the mountain."

> *"So be your name Buxbaum or Bixby or Bray*
> *or Mordecai Ali Van Allen O'Shea*
> *You're off to Great Places!*
> *Today is your day!*
> *Your mountain is waiting.*
> *So... get on your way!*
>
> **—Dr. Seuss**

78

GOT A BONE TO PICK?

"I have had enough, Lord," he said. "Take my life."
—1 Kings 19:4

𝕴 LOST MY JOB. WELL, OK, I have lost several jobs, but it was never my fault. Those bosses had issues. It hurt. People I cared for have gotten sick, injured and died. It was sad and wrong. Life shouldn't be that way. My girlfriend broke up with me. Well, OK, several girlfriends have broken up with me. But they had issues. I cried over one of them. OK maybe a few times. Lightning hit the house once and I jumped three feet off my chair. It fried several expensive appliances I didn't have the money to replace. No, I didn't believe in insurance, but that shouldn't have happened anyway. Why did God pick on my house?

Have you ever gotten angry and all bent out of shape? There was a time in my life when I blamed God for every bad thing that happened. I hated Him sometimes.

Forrest: "Still no shrimp, Lieutenant Dan."
Lt. Dan Taylor: "Okay, so I was wrong."
Forrest: "Well, how are we going to find them?"
Lt. Dan Taylor: "Well, maybe you should just pray for shrimp."
Forrest [voice-over]: "So I went to church every Sunday. Sometimes Lieutenant Dan came too, though I think he left the praying up to me."
[Another catch of junk is dumped onto the deck.]

Forrest: "No shrimp."

Lt. Dan Taylor: "Where the #%@'s this God of yours?"*

Forrest [voice-over]: "It's funny Lieutenant Dan said that, 'cause right then ... God showed up."

[On the boat deck during a hurricane]

Forrest [voice-over]: "Now me, I was scared. But Lieutenant Dan, he was mad."

Lt. Dan Taylor: "Come on! You call this a storm? Blow! You son of a #$%^and! Blow! It's time for a showdown! Just you and me! I'm right here! Come and get me!"*

[We then see news footage that Hurricane Carmen wiped out Bayou La Batre's entire shrimping fleet except for Forrest's ship, the Jenny.]

Forrest [voice-over]: "After that, shrimpin' was easy."

[Forrest and Lt. Dan are working on the boat]

Lt. Dan Taylor: "Forrest, I never thanked you for saving my life."

[Lieutenant Dan pulls himself out of his chair to the railing and jumps into the ocean. He swims into the setting sun.]

Forrest [voice-over]: He never actually said so, but I think he made his peace with God.

—Forrest Gump

Let me ask you a question: Do you have a score to settle with God before you will really trust Him for everything? If you do, don't be afraid to holler at Him.

I think God likes honest, intimate communication with you in any form He can get it. I also think the more passionate, the better. Talk to Him about your fears, your anger, your hopes and dreams. Make it real, drop it at His feet, and then get over it. God wants to help you put down this baggage and get past it, so you can carry out His mission on earth.

"When you come to your wit's end, that's where God lives."

—Frank Thomas, one of my many fathers

79

THE RETIRED CEO

"Success means using your knowledge and experience to satisfy yourself. Significance means using your knowledge and experience to change the lives of others."

—Bob Buford

I SOLD REAL ESTATE to talented retired guys who went crazy without an end game. Many people were dragged along with them. Larry is the guy who comes clearly and immediately to mind.

There were many "Larrys" where I worked as a real estate broker, but this one guy stands out. He and his wife came to central Texas after a long, successful career. He'd been the CEO of a big corporation overseas, in charge of everything and everyone. He was doing just what he loved, and he was in control.

Then, one day it was over. Larry took the pension and the "golden parachute." Time to retire and build the dream home they'd always wanted.

I sold them two lots in a gated community overlooking a golf course. They hired an architect and drew up the biggest monster retirement house you've ever seen.

Larry was a builder's nightmare. He arrived every day at 7:30 a.m. on the construction site and wouldn't leave until six in the evening. He didn't have anything else to do with his time.

Larry fussed over trim work and argued about floor tile alignment. He ordered the subcontractors around and noticed minor defects in the paint job. (What are "spider cracks" in concrete, anyway?) Larry could turn a happy eight-hour day into what seemed thirty-seven hours of torturing the working man, just by being there to save himself a nickel. He seemed to revel in making people miserable.

"And as your business prospered, Ebenezer Scrooge, a golden idol took possession of your heart."

—Charles Dickens, A Christmas Carol

Nobody liked seeing Larry's car pull up. Two electricians, three plumbers, a painter, and the garage door installer all quit over Larry's insulting, bossy comments. His wife and the builder didn't like it, but they hadn't much to gain by challenging him. So they made themselves scarce when they could.

Then it was the patio guys, the alarm guys, the swimming pool contractor, the landscaper, and the guy who installed the outdoor sound system in the flower beds. The speakers were supposed to be plastic rocks, not frogs.

Finally, it was finished. That is, right after Larry stiffed the builder on the last chunk of change because the punch list wasn't complete. There was this one piece of crown molding way up in the corner of the thirty-foot ceiling that wasn't caulked just right.

Then it was done, and the big house was quiet ... too quiet. Larry drank more than normal, slept more than normal, ate more than normal, and hollered more than normal. Sometimes he tangled with the homeowners' association. Someone's grandkid had a jalopy that leaked oil, way down the street from Larry's million-dollar house. He didn't like the car or the spot on the pavement. The entrance security gate opened too slowly. It was always something.

The handwriting was on the wall when Larry called me to ask about real estate prices in the neighborhood. I sold the house for sixty percent of what they had put into it, less than a year after they moved in. Larry got half of that when the divorce was settled. They say the marriage had mostly gone well when Larry was working, but the Mrs. had had just about enough of retirement, at least with Larry. Apparently she now lives a quiet and happy life somewhere in Spain.

Do you think proactively pouring love into and gaining significance out of a retirement life full of missions activity might have helped Larry and his wife be happy? Maybe not, but I sure wish guys like him would give it a try. Just think of what God could do with all that energy!

What are you doing to other people this week? Er…I mean what are you doing for other people this week? ❧

"Each of you should use whatever gift you have received to serve others, as faithful stewards of God's grace in its various forms."
—1 Peter 4:10

80

THE GOOD OL' BOY SYNDROME

"I never did nothing to nobody."

—Frank Lopez in Scarface

THE GOOD OL' BOY can be anyone, man or woman, old or young, from virtually any walk of life. They've worked hard and deserve to rest if they want. They're not hurting anyone, but they're not helping much either. Most of the good ol' boys I refer to are retired.

Quick! Can you point to the Scripture that says we give up working completely when we make enough money? Don't think so. That's an American myth.

"I'm not ready to take up the rockin' chair."

—Augustus McCrea in Lonesome Dove

It is not necessarily what they look like or how they dress, their education or personal habits that make them good ol' boys (or gals). It can be anybody anywhere. What distinguishes these people is a focus on self which permeates their being and is evident if you observe how they fill their days for any length of time. It is in how they go about having fun and what they get involved in on a regular basis. It is how they acquire a sense of identity and gather self-worth.

I hate golf, by the way. Just sayin'. It's a fun pastime, and I play from time to time. However, I find few obsessions in the world that bleed more time, talent, and treasure out of people. It renders them idle and indifferent to helping others. To me golf is comparable to the drug trade. Millions of people are intoxicated and distracted at enormous expense. We could solve a ton of problems in the Lord's service if retirees alone gave up this game and redirected their lives and resources toward missions. I'm sorry, I know you love it. I like it too. I've just seen too many children without homes or schools, and too many sick or injured without care.

Picture a car in neutral with the motor running. It is not going backward, it's just not going forward.

The good ol' boy may donate money to missions, the symphony, children's hospitals, his church, the zoo, the local food shelter, etc., but he is not personally or actively involved. His check suffices, if he feels like writing it. He doesn't have any skin in the game; nothing's at stake.

The good ol' boy may be a Christian and may regularly attend church. Yet, even though he believes all or part of the Bible is God's Word, he doesn't feel obligated to answer the call to missions.

All I can do is keep putting it in front of people. Our mission is not only a biblical obligation; it is something that will bring us endless joy, significance, and satisfaction. It can be the greatest sport we've ever played. An outward focus helps people and brings joy to God and ourselves in the process.

I encourage you good ol' boys to find your mission. Hint: It's not at the nineteenth hole! ❧

"Deep in man's heart are some fundamental questions that simply cannot be answered at the kitchen table. Who am I? What am I made of? What am I destined for? It is fear that keeps a man at home where things are neat and orderly and under his control. But the answers to his deepest questions are not to be found on television or in the refrigerator."

—John Eldredge, Wild at Heart

81

BUT WHO AM I?

"Though he be but little, he is fierce."
—William Shakespeare

YOU MIGHT LOVE THE LORD, but maybe you are asking yourself this question right now: How can I convince some guy down the street, or around the world, to become a disciple of Christ? Me, someone who may not go to church every week or has a flimsy grasp of the Bible at best. How could I get a complete stranger to pay attention to and obey what Jesus has commanded, let alone baptize them? Who am I to do that?

Pea Eye Parker: "They're gonna try sneakin' up on us in the dark, ain't they Gus?"
Augustus McCrea: "Be takin' a chance if they do, couple of sharp-shooters like us."
Pea Eye Parker: "I ain't no sharp-shooter! I usually miss if I ain't got time to take careful aim."
Augustus McCrea: "By God but it's depressin' to talk to you, Pea."
—Lonesome Dove

The simple answer is, permit God to do it through you. Allow the Holy Spirit and the love of Christ to flow through you in whatever way comes naturally. It's as easy as falling off a log.

Just go, share what you know, and learn; God will do the rest. Remember well what Jesus said:

"Follow me, and I will make you fishers of men"
—Matthew 4:19

The words will come later. Don't worry about that until it feels more natural, because if you just follow the Lord, He will **make you** a fisher of men. Don't think for a moment He can't. The apostles were uneducated fishermen.

Just follow. Freely give people your time, talent, and treasure. When you show them that their problems and well-being mean something to you, it becomes much easier to share this message from Jesus. When you show people they have a friend in you, a real friend, they will want to hear more of what you have to say about that book you're carrying.

I don't play the guitar or sing very well. I'm not a doctor, a builder, or a door-to-door evangelist, but I have learned about and worked beside all of them. I am personally gifted as a guide and facilitator for all these mission types. I match the resources with the needs and put them together. I inspire people to get involved.

Step up to the plate and take a swing. It doesn't matter what you know how to do or where you're comfortable sharing it. Just do it. You'll be amazed at where God may take you. My first time sharing the Lord deliberately was something else.

"For it is God who works in you to will and to act in order to fulfill his good purpose."

—Philippians 2:13

82

THE UNWILLING WITNESS

"I bet there's rich folks eatin' in a fancy dining car.
They're probably drinkin' coffee, and smokin' big cigars.
But I know I had it comin'. I know I can't be free.
But those people keep a movin',
And that's what tortures me."

—Johnny Cash, "Folsom Prison Blues

I WENT TO PRISON ONCE.

They didn't lock me up for long, because I was just visiting, but I got a feel for it. This wasn't just any old prison either. This was Garcia Moreno Maximum Security Prison in Quito, Ecuador. It was the deepest, darkest, most horror-filled dungeon I ever could have imagined. I had no idea what I was getting into, and the experience changed me forever.

I wasn't a Christian in 1995, didn't even really understand the concept of accepting Christ as my personal Savior. It's not the Catholic way. I knew God was there, and I prayed once in a while, especially if I was having a hard time (see story on HAT YAI). It was a fair-weather relationship. I went to church occasionally, often just sitting alone quietly in an empty cathedral.

It came to pass I attended a small "gringo" church in Quito one Sunday, and Pastor Chris invited me to visit the foreign inmates in prison with him. It sounded like an adventure, so I went.

My first impression as we approached the creepy, stadium-sized lockup gave me a memorable snapshot of who was running the place. We passed through the main gate in a fence fortified with razor wire, then crossed a sprawling cobblestone courtyard. Two uniformed guards escorted a filthy, bedraggled prisoner wearing rags that hung on his skinny body. We followed as they cursed and roughed him up, his long, greasy hair flopping about as they shook him. Chris and I passed them on our way to the prison entrance, and I got a look at his face. Blood trickling out of a gash in the man's cheek, he mumbled in protest before the guards pushed him down in unison. He fell with such force that his face impacted the cobblestones without his hands having time to come up for any protection at all. I can never forget the punishing splat sound it made. All the poor guy did was gurgle.

I froze instantly, staring at this now unconscious man. His blood poured out in little streams as the guards howled with laughter. They hoisted the motionless heap up again, his face unrecognizable from just moments before. He was a bloody mess. Strands of his black, unruly hair hung loosely around his face, and his teeth were broken and scattered about his lips. I could not tell if he had survived or not. (Years later when I saw the movie The Passion of the Christ, I thought of this man during the scene when a bleeding Jesus dragged His cross amidst the abusive crowd.)

The guards stopped, noticing my horrified stare. Fortunately Chris came back, grabbed my arm, wished them a "Muy buenos dias," and hurriedly escorted me away. I'd never seen real brutality before and kept looking back in disbelief as I was whisked across the yard.

Then we went inside. We were frisked, scrutinized, and marked on the back of the hand with an indelible Marks-A-

Lot before being permitted through two sets of barred gates and guards carrying machine guns. This checkpoint was called La Boca, or The Mouth. They had big rings of long iron keys. The clank of the locks turning and the squeak of the gate opening were eerie, and I think the guards really enjoyed watching us jump when they slammed those bars shut behind us. We wouldn't be coming out unless they said so.

The last thing the guy said to us with a smile was, "No lava sus manos," or "Don't wash your hands." The mark of the Marks-A-Lot was our ticket back out. Even though I knew I could get out later, I instinctively started planning how I might break out of that terrible place.

Max: "Catch the Midnight Express."
Billy Haynes: "But what's that?"
Max: "Well, it's not a train. It's a prison word for … escape. But it doesn't stop around here."

—Midnight Express

A freight train could have driven through the dark, cavernous, stone-walled tunnel, and I couldn't see a light at the end of it. As we proceeded downward, ominous noises emitted from deep within, and a foul stench assaulted our nostrils. They called the tunnel La Garganta, or The Throat. I had little doubt it was just that, and we were walking down into the belly of the beast. Dread shrouded every corner, and trepidation weighed on me heavily. Whatever was in there, we were past the point of no return, and we were going in to get up close and personal.

We proceeded to a circular hub where several hundred people were wandering around. Cell-block hallways led off in every direction, each block being three caged levels high. Inmates didn't have orange or striped uniforms like in the States; they wore the clothes they arrived in. There were women and children everywhere, because Saturday was visitors day. In an open prison population, inmates move around freely with the public. There was not a uniformed guard in sight. We were literally diving into the pool with the masses.

Chris took my hand. "Don't look directly at anyone, and don't stop to talk. Stick close to me and keep moving." I was only too happy to oblige as he led me through the throng, and when I wasn't holding his hand, I was holding onto his shirt like my mama's apron strings.

We passed rows of cells which resembled small dorm rooms and businesses. Some were wood carving shops, others held tailors repairing clothes. I saw shoe repair, an electronics and watch shop, a small grocer, and several restaurant stalls, all inside the prison cells of inmates. Everybody had weapons. I saw no firearms, but there was everything from knives and machetes to needles and kitchen utensils. I felt like an alien from another planet. Hawkers, hucksters, and homosexuals all hollered for us to come in for a visit, and many touched or tried to grab us as we passed. Chris politely but firmly plowed through with me in tow.

We proceeded to the third level and down a long row of cells. Chris greeted people here and there. He stopped at a restaurant in one of the cells and ordered lunch for ten people. He paid in sucres, then turned to me and said, "I hope you like Mexican food. This is the best in Quito." I didn't believe him, and couldn't imagine this was even allowed in prison. It was a scary thought.

White faces appeared out of the last four cells, and Chris made the introductions. I don't remember any of their names, but all were young guys from the U.S. and Europe who had

been busted for drug trafficking in the Quito airport. (In Ecuador 1994, whether you were caught with a gram or a bale of cocaine, you got the same sentence: eight years. Judges enjoyed rubber-stamping those they snagged as international drug traffickers, because it showed they were on the job.)

They'd all been caught by the airport "Lie Detector." Oh, it wasn't a machine. The Lie Detector was a scary woman in airport security who acted like a machine. She had short red hair and a very serious military presence. One guy characterized her as similar to Rosa Klebb, one of James Bond's adversaries in the movie *From Russia with Love*. Anybody the airport staff deemed suspicious was sent to this woman. She sat across the table from her subject, insisted they hold her hands tightly, and looked deep into their eyes during questioning.

All the gringos in the prison nodded when the procedure was described. They shook uncontrollably in the interrogation, unable to maintain eye contact as instructed. The Lie Detector then gave a nod, and a dozen machine-gun-carrying guards entered with dogs. They were surrounded, roughly strip-searched, their bags torn apart, and the hidden contraband found. Naked beatings were the standard welcome into their new world order.

They all professed to be "mules," people who carry drugs for a larger organization. These guys didn't find the rich, highlife their handlers had described to them.

"Cause a year from now, when you're kickin' it in the Caribbean, you're gonna say to yourself, "Marcellus Wallace was right!"

—Pulp Fiction

Things hadn't worked out as planned.

Our Mexican food was delivered to picnic tables out on the "veranda," a fenced concrete rooftop. Chris prayed then said, "Where's that new guy?" One of the eight gringos had not come out of his cell in the hour we'd been there, and somebody went to call him for lunch. I may forget everyone else, but for as long as I live, I will never forget Peyton Kamden Reed.

He had reddish-blond hair, emerald-green eyes, and a slightly freckled young face. He nodded slightly in our direction and sat at the far end of the table with barely a hello as we all started eating. The guys told us Peyton had only been there about three weeks, another notch in the Lie Detector's belt. He kept to himself and rarely spoke unless required. He was twenty-three years old and still in a state of shock and depression over becoming their neighbor for the next eight years of his life in the "Quito Hilton."

The guys chatted at my end of the table and asked us all sorts of questions about ourselves and the world outside. When asked what I was doing in Ecuador, I explained I was a scuba diving and wildlife guide in the Galapagos Islands.

Peyton lit up like a pinball machine. "Really? Wow! I'm a diver too! What do you do? Where do you live? What kind of ships do you use out there? Do you use a dive computer? What millimeter neoprene do you have to wear? Have you seen a volcanic eruption? What marine life do you see in the ocean around the islands?"

This went on for quite a few minutes, and I could scarcely get a mouthful of Mexican food before Peyton shot me another excited question. His fellow inmates expressed surprise, even joy, at seeing this boy emerge from his shell for the first time. Once you go in, you become part of the "familia," and these guys had been worried about their new little brother. "Amazing!" one of them spouted. "This guy hasn't said twenty words since he got here almost a month ago, and now look at him."

Chris suggested I move my plate to the other end of the table so I could chat with Peyton more easily. I began asking him about his life. He lived on Grand Cayman and worked as a dive master, guiding tours. His American fiancée had gone home for a couple of weeks. It was then he'd been approached by a narcotics trafficker and asked to make a "quick run" to Ecuador. Peyton planned to buy a house and raise a family with the money this one drug transaction could produce. He had it all figured out.

"I've been to Cayman," I said, trying to establish better rapport. "What boat did you work on?"

He smiled broadly, and his eyes twinkled. "The Lady Kate, a fine, big Hatteras. She sleeps eight people and can make it over to Little Cayman and Cayman Brac." He started to go on about the other features, when I broke in with a grin.

"I know the Lady Kate! That's Ken Covington's boat! I'm best buddies with his son Kenny! You've probably met them. I know your captain, Clayton Eubanks, and that crazy deckhand Ashlan! We went diving one time!" I thought it was so cool, and what a small world.

Small world indeed! Peyton was snuffed out like a candle. The smile and bright energy were gone. He visibly shook as his face reddened, his eyes darting all around. His mouth moved, but nothing came out except a moan as tears swelled in his eyes and rolled over his freckled cheeks. Peyton dropped his fork on the floor and bolted from the table, crying hysterically, making a beeline back to the cell block.

"What did you say to him, man?" I turned to face angry inmates staring me down. One, on his feet and visibly upset, said in an aggressive tone, "Yeah, man, what did you say?"

"I don't know. I just said I knew the people who owned the boat he works on. I don't know what happened."

They all seemed to chill out. "Oh," one said. "I get it. You know his people. That's bizarre. How do you know people there?" I shrugged, and they all nodded at something I didn't understand yet.

"Peyton hasn't told anyone. Nobody knows he's here. His friends didn't even know he went to Ecuador. It was going to be his secret. His girlfriend doesn't know. His employer and the crew don't know. He hasn't even told his parents back in Aberdeen. He's too afraid and ashamed to tell them, and now you step right into his world. You know them. You're here. You know he's here. That's why he's freaked. You just blew his mind, and he doesn't know what to say. He probably thinks you're going to squeal."

"I'm really sorry." I felt so helpless. "I didn't mean to hurt his feelings … but you mean his parents don't even know what happened? Surely they've filed a missing persons report or something. They probably think he's dead."

The lightbulb suddenly turned on in Pastor Chris at the other end of the table. He got up and darted over as soon as he'd absorbed the full picture. "This is it, Steve! You gotta get in there, man! Right now!" he demanded with a crazed look on his face.

"What?! Are you out of your mind? I just upset the guy! I'm not going in there!"

"Don't you see, Steve? This is a divine appointment! The Holy Spirit's in this thing! God sent you here! I can feel it! You've got to get in there and witness to the guy right now!" Chris was trying to get me up on my feet, but I wasn't budging. My initial reaction was Chris had suffered a mental/spiri-

tual breakdown in the midst of this unusual and emotionally charged drama.

"What kind of appointment? A divine what? Witness?! What are you talking about? What does that even mean?" At the time, I was oblivious to the meaning of the word outside the realm of a courtroom. Chris was now speaking a language with which I was not the least bit familiar or comfortable.

"Look!" he said, staring directly into my eyes. "This guy's in real trouble. Look around this place, for God's sake! You're the first person he's really opened up to since he got here. His people are worried sick about him for sure. They don't know where he is! He looks suicidal, Steve! Don't you think it's a little weird that God put you in here today? You're a diver. He's a diver. You have things in common. And now you magically know his captain and crew somehow? What's up with that?"

"I don't know what's up, Chris. Just a strange coincidence, I guess."

"It's not a coincidence! You're here for a reason!"

"Now take a deep breath," he said, taking one himself and calming a bit, which calmed me. "Understand you have been sent here for a reason, and you have a chance to help this guy out right now. Take it easy, go in there, and sit with him. Talk to him. Say a prayer, tell him God loves him—whatever comes onto your heart. Don't just sit here, brother, please. You could save Peyton's life. This is the reason you're here today."

It didn't make any sense to me, but I knew he was right. I couldn't just sit there. We could hear Peyton sobbing violently inside his cell. I don't remember ever being more scared about something. This had suddenly turned from a sightseeing tour into as real as it gets. I gathered up all the courage I could muster and walked into his cell.

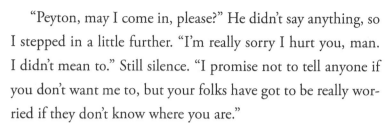

"Peyton, may I come in, please?" He didn't say anything, so I stepped in a little further. "I'm really sorry I hurt you, man. I didn't mean to." Still silence. "I promise not to tell anyone if you don't want me to, but your folks have got to be really worried if they don't know where you are."

He sat up in his bunk. "I can't tell my father," he finally blubbered between powerful sobs. I've never seen a grown man cry so hard. We talked about his plans to marry, and how that was likely over. His job, his life in Cayman, and everything he'd worked so hard for were gone in a flash. Now he was in this dungeon, and he couldn't see survival as an option. Life itself appeared over to Peyton. The guys outside were right. He was thinking about suicide. This seemed to beat telling his father what he'd done and where he was.

If there was ever a time in my selfish little life I really and truly felt for someone other than myself, it was at that moment. I felt the deepest sympathy for Peyton Kamden Reed of Aberdeen, Scotland. I cry every time I think about it, and that was over twenty years ago. I didn't care how foolish or awkward I felt. I didn't care where I was or who heard me. I didn't care that I didn't know what to do or say. I was going to do whatever I could do to help this guy. I couldn't solve his problems, but

I did what I could. We were in a terrible situation, in a remote corner of a horrible place, in a country far from home.

There was only one thing to do. I didn't say anything to Peyton. I just knelt down on the concrete floor beside his rusty bunk like we used to do at bedtime when I was a little boy. I put my elbows on the bed, hands clasped tightly together, and began to pray what I knew. I started with, "Our Father, who art in heaven" and went from there. I got through the Lord's Prayer, the Hail Mary, and the Catholic Profession of Faith, then had to roll on my own.

I cracked my eyes open at one point, and Peyton had knelt at the other end of the bunk, eyes and hands tightly clenched and tears streaming down his face. Nobody had ever taught me more than rote-memory prayer, but the situation called for me to keep going, so I did. I prayed for safety. I prayed for peace. I prayed for a miracle to get him out of there. I prayed and babbled on quite a while, covering everything I could think of. Then I stopped and stayed silent for what seemed like the longest time, as the glow of a powerful spiritual feeling subsided in me. For a time I forgot where I was, and then I was crying bitterly.

"But you will receive power when the Holy Spirit comes on you; and you will be my witnesses in Jerusalem, and in all Judea and Samaria, and to the ends of the earth."

—Acts 1:8

I finally opened my eyes, and Peyton was sitting on the bed. He was not smiling, to be sure, but there was clearly more brightness about him. He was no longer panicked or crying, which was definitely an improvement. I realized then that the power of prayer and God's presence had given him real and visible hope. Maybe for the first time since his arrest, the future didn't look quite so dark for Peyton. I began to suspect that maybe Pastor Chris was right: God really had sent me there and used me personally. How could that be possible?

Pastor Chris came in with all the guys, who had been listening at the cell door. It's a tight community. Handshakes, hugs, and even cheers went all around. We celebrated God in the dungeon.

Peyton brought me a piece of paper with his parents' address and asked me to tell them. He just didn't know what to say. Before long they were writing to each other, communicating more than they had in years. Pastor Chris brought him and other inmates Bibles, and Peyton apparently accepted Christ and became a student of the Word long before I ever did.

Peyton was released and went back home after doing three years in Garcia Moreno Prison. I lost touch with him, but I will never forget what happened and what was revealed to me when we knelt and prayed together. Deliberate, open prayer and witnessing are powerful. The world needs folks who will share the love of Christ and pray with others.

Have you ever had a moment when prayer was the only solution? If not, just wait. You will. ❧

"Then they cried out to the Lord in their trouble, and he brought them out of their distress. He stilled the storm to a whisper; the waves of the sea were hushed. They were glad when it grew calm, and he guided them to their desired haven."

—Psalm 107:28-30

83

THE McFLY SYNDROME

OU HAVE NOTHING to offer in missions? If I had a nickel for every time I heard that one! I don't believe you. Go tell it to someone else. If you tell me you have nothing to offer on a mission trip, then I'll tell you one of several things.

I might tell you that you don't understand enough about missionary service. A major component of your going is … you are going. You get involved. Rest assured, I could probably accomplish more physically if you just gave me the money for your plane ticket and I hired local people to do the work rather than you coming along. However, if you think this way you miss the point completely. It's not nearly as much about any project as it is about your direct and deliberate involvement. You have to therefore, go and be available where God can reveal things to you.

"Be available to God. When you know, you must go."

—Debbie Witherspoon

The major benefit to the mission team is that you want to be part of the team. Maybe you'd like to go it alone or with a friend or two. No problem. The point is, by going, you get exposed to what it's all about, and the Lord touches you in the process. You must therefore, go if you are able.

Butch: "Next time I say, 'Let's go someplace like Bolivia,' let's go someplace like Bolivia!"
Sundance: "Yeah. Next time."
—Butch Cassidy and the Sundance Kid

Your self-esteem may be hovering too low. Caution: You may be suffering from the dreaded "McFly Syndrome":

What if they say I'm no good? What if they say, "Get outta here, kid. You got no future"? I mean, I just don't think I can take that kind of rejection."
—Marty McFly in Back to the Future

Guide your plane to a higher level. Any thoughts that you have nothing to offer are beneath you. You're worthy of more. Take a fresh inventory of your God-given talents and life experiences. You know things and have special gifts the Lord can use.

We serve in countries where people have limited knowledge of things you've known for years. Basic first aid, for instance. When you were a kid your parents probably taught you if you get a cut or scrape, you just clean it off, dab it with an antibiotic ointment, and slap a Band-Aid on it. In southern Peru I once helped a man who didn't know this and was about to get gangrene in his infected leg from what had originally been an unclean minor injury. Your knowledge is valuable, but you may not think so because it is commonplace in the US.

Take another look in the mirror, friend. See what God sees, and ask yourself this question: Why was I one of the lucky ones born into a place of more privilege than the rest of the world? Because you were chosen to share the abundance. That's why.

Don't be surprised if you get out there on a mission trip and God shows you things about yourself you never knew. Go on a trip and let Him touch you.

"Don't ask what the world needs. Ask what makes you come alive, and go do it. Because what the world needs are people who have come alive."

—Howard Thurman

Everybody knows something about something. Did you ever bathe a child or mop a floor? Can you teach, draw a picture, or play a game? Can you drive a car? You may not be a doctor or dentist, but could you hold the light while one helps somebody? Did you ever mix concrete or swing a hammer? Play a guitar, sing a song, give a hug, or just walk quietly beside people who want to show you their home or village? There are plenty of ways to show other people how Jesus loves us. Are you willing?

"If all I can do is put a Band-Aid on someone. I'm sharing the Love of Christ."

—Gina Holland – Missionary

Maybe you are an architect, engineer, or general contractor. Maybe you know about plumbing, electrical, roofing, water wells, or … anything. Do you have any idea how badly people around the world need you? I can tell many stories of people who said they were not coming on a mission trip because they had nothing to offer, And infact had just what was needed.. These folks crack me up.

First was Ruth. Ruth "didn't have anything to offer." It would be a waste of her time and money, and she would just be a burden to the rest of the team. She was in her twenties and had been raised on a farm. "I'd like to go with this sports team from my church," she shyly admitted. "I have some friends going, but I don't play sports or speak Spanish. So I'm not going. There won't be anything for me to do, but thanks anyway."

After talking to Ruth awhile, I found out her parents' farm produced thirty different kinds of jam, jelly, and salsa. She seemed to come alive when she described the pH balance required for pickled vegetables and homemade hot sauce. She knew all about the preserving process. Ruth went on the trip and was responsible for helping local people learn how to make money by preserving their own produce.

Second was Danny. Danny had "nothing to offer." He came on a trip but hung on the sidelines. His team taught English in our school, but he just watched. Danny worked for a cement plant and drove a concrete delivery truck. I noticed him the second day watching me lay bricks for a barbecue pit project. (A pig farm supported the orphanage, and I needed a way to cook pork for guests.) He laughed when I told him my design idea. He knew all about this stuff. By the time Danny got finished, we had a first-class smoker. He had come alive!

Third was Glynda. Glynda "didn't have anything to offer." She was the biggest hoot of all! This little woman in her sixties seemed totally depressed when I asked her what she thought she might do on a teachers' mission trip. Her idea was to hang around and help the others, but she was thinking of not going at all. "I'll probably just be in the way," I remember her saying, very dejected.

So I started asking her about hobbies or things she liked to do. Well, she didn't have anything except reading. She didn't do much. I really thought I was going to lose her. Glynda was used to staying home anyway.

Then we struck pay dirt. I asked her what she did for a living. "Oh, I work for the Civil Air Patrol." I didn't really even know what that was. "So, you're a pilot?" I quizzed.

"Oh no, I'm just an administrator," she said shyly, but her tone lifted a notch. "We're in contact with pilots all over the United States. It's an organization that started in World War II."

Then I pounced. "So you like planes, pilots, and all that stuff, Glynda?"

She instantly had come alive. "Oh yes! My job doesn't pay much, but I love it. I don't fly, of course, but I get to be near planes, meet pilots, find out where everybody's going, talk on the radio, and all that. It's really fun."

Gotcha! "So, Glynda," I said, "how about instead of you tagging along with the English or math teachers on this trip, you create your own workshop on, say, aircraft? You could talk about different planes and how they work, and maybe inspire some of these Peruvian kids to be pilots one day. What do you think?"

There was a long silence on the other end of the phone, then Glynda went off like a bottle rocket. "Wow! You really think I could do that? Wow! That would be so much fun! Why, I could do this and bring this and try this ..."

She was the biggest inspirational hit of anyone we ever hosted. The kids talked about her for years afterward. Glynda's theme for her mission to Peru was "God made air for more than breathing." She brought homemade aircraft kits for rockets, planes, and hovercraft. She taught our kids about propulsion and lift. She encouraged them that if they used the gifts God gave them and worked hard in math and science, they could be pilots someday. She was the most amazing teacher of all.

You say you have nothing to offer in missions? I say Come Alive and you will! ✺

"Our deepest fear is not that we are inadequate. Our deepest fear is that we are powerful beyond measure. It is our light, not our darkness, that most frightens us. We ask ourselves, Who am I to be brilliant, gorgeous, talented, fabulous? Actually, who are you not to be? You are a child of God. Your playing small doesn't serve the world. There's nothing enlightened about shrinking so that other people won't feel insecure around you. We are all meant to shine, as children do. We were born to make manifest the glory of God that is within us. It's not just in some of us; it's in everyone. And as we let our own light shine, we unconsciously give other people permission to do the same. As we're liberated from our own fear, our presence automatically liberates others."

—*Inauguration Speech of Nelson Mandela*

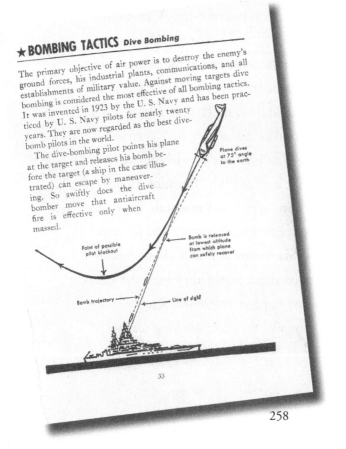

★ BOMBING TACTICS Dive Bombing

The primary objective of air power is to destroy the enemy's ground forces, his industrial plants, communications, and all establishments of military value. Against moving targets dive bombing is considered the most effective of all bombing tactics. It was invented in 1923 by the U. S. Navy and has been practiced by U. S. Navy pilots for nearly twenty years. They are now regarded as the best dive-bomb pilots in the world.

The dive-bombing pilot points his plane at the target and releases his bomb before the target (a ship in the case illustrated) can escape by maneuvering. So swiftly does the dive bomber move that antiaircraft fire is effective only when massed.

Plane dives at 75° angle to the earth

Point of possible pilot blackout

Bomb is released at lowest altitude from which plane can safely recover

Bomb trajectory

Line of sight

33

84

NOT QUALIFIED

"It is possible for the most obscure person in a church, with a heart right toward God, to exercise as much power for the evangelization of the world, as it is for those who stand in the most prominent positions."

—John R. Mott

I GROW VERY TIRED of the advanced Bible students who tell us "laymen" that we are not qualified to be missionaries. I urge you, do not be discouraged by these people. They usually mean well.

The fact is, most of us ordinary believers have not spent our entire lives in classrooms reading books, writing papers, and giving lectures about the contents and meaning of the Bible. That doesn't mean we aren't supposed to go serve in missions. Don't believe it for a second!

Overcoming the World Missions Crisis, edited by Russell L. Penney, has both encouraged and discouraged me at the same time. It is a superior book on missions, to be sure, full of heartfelt wisdom. I encourage you to buy and study it in depth.

On one hand, this book has encouraged me to be a better student of theology. It is, after all, only in our formal education, study of the Bible, and exchange with other believers and teachers that we get better at sharing God's message. I couldn't agree more that the better educated the missionary, the better he can teach the gospel and develop strong believers. There is no question about this.

On the other hand, I have been discouraged at how the book portrays the missionary who may not have extensive training to preach and teach the Bible. At least we have the courage and obedience to follow the Lord's calling into a foreign land and introduce it to someone. Chapter 9 condescendingly refers to "chop and chatter" missionaries, carrying Bibles and hacking their way through the jungle with machetes as they chatter about the Bible without much formal training. This is me, I'm afraid, but I'm doing the best I can.

We attract and guide hundreds of people into the mission field. We support and build churches, orphanages, and schools that teach the gospel. We have shared the love of Christ and brought His resources to bear in so many ways. We and those like us have been the long-term support team for numerous resourceful missionary talents. We've "carried the water."

I truly have the deepest respect for highly educated missionaries, their ability to teach the Bible, and the lifelong learning essential to missions development and effectiveness. However, I respectfully disagree with the idea that the majority of lesser-educated but lionhearted Christians with their vast array of gifts and skills have a lesser place in the mission field. Try to tell that to the multitude of missionary foot soldiers beside whom we serve.

"From Berlin, Rome, and Tokyo, we have been described as
a nation of weaklings—'playboys'—who would hire British
soldiers, or Russian soldiers, or Chinese soldiers to do our fighting
for us. Let them repeat that now! Let them tell that to General
MacArthur and his men. Let them tell that to the sailors who
today are hitting hard in the far waters of the Pacific. Let them
tell that to the boys in the Flying Fortresses. Let them tell that to
the Marines!"

—Franklin D. Roosevelt

Many people require repeated exposure to the love of Christ before they will even open a Bible, have a deep conversation, or attend church. Were it not for your "chop and chatter" missionary, I daresay many thousands, if not millions, of unreached people never would have been attracted to a church or formal classes where they could grow. We need as many missionaries in the field as we can possibly get. Bible "experts" are often the guys getting the sweet church jobs back home, never to be seen in the field. Those who do come out of the church and into the field make up only one important part of a much larger missions team out there.

Feeding, watering, and nurturing new Christian growth is clearly of vital importance. But somebody's got to plant the seeds in the first place. We all have a role, as Paul wrote:

> *What, after all, is Apollos? And what is Paul? Only servants, through whom you came to believe—as the Lord has assigned to each his task. I planted the seed, Apollos watered it, but God has been making it grow. So neither the one who plants nor the one who waters is anything, but only God, who makes things grow. The one who plants and the one who waters have one purpose, and they will each be rewarded according to their own labor. For we are co-workers in God's service; you are God's field, God's building.*
> **—1 Corinthians 3:5-9**

Teddy Roosevelt couldn't get a formally trained U.S. Army regiment to command in the Spanish-American War. So he formed the Rough Riders, the untrained, uncouth rabble who took San Juan Hill in the most famous battle of the war. Roosevelt's approach, in his own words, was, "Do what you can, with what you have, where you are."

That's what we're doing. The world and God's work in it are big, and we need every hand on deck. By all means, get as educated as you can, but for God's sake friend, don't obsess over your lack of formal qualifications and let that stop you from carrying out your mission.

"Believe you can and you're halfway there."
—*Theodore Roosevelt*

And don't let any discouraging naysayer rain on your circus and stop you either. Again, the words of Teddy Roosevelt offer encouragement:

"It is not the critic who counts; not the man who points out how the strong man stumbles, or where the doer of deeds could have done them better. The credit belongs to the man who is actually in the arena, whose face is marred by dust and sweat and blood; who strives valiantly; who errs, who comes short again and again, because there is no effort without error and shortcoming; but who does actually strive to do the deeds; who knows great enthusiasms, the great devotions; who spends himself in a worthy cause; who at the best knows in the end the triumph of high achievement, and who at the worst, if he fails, at least fails while daring greatly, so that his place shall never be with those cold and timid souls who neither know victory nor defeat."

You've got what it takes for your unique, God-given role in missions. It is clearly your biblical obligation and will be among the greatest joys of your life. Believe, and walk boldly in it.

Therefore, we will all go—wherever we're called, with whatever we've got.

What have you got and where are you going?

85

SPIRITUAL WARFARE

*"Good morning, I'm Roger Grimsby. Today, the entire Eastern
Seaboard is alive with talk of incidents of paranormal activity.
Alleged ghost sightings and related supernatural occurrences have
been reported across the entire Tri-State area."*

—Ghostbusters

I SHARED WITH A FRIEND how many problems we were
having in the months before we went to the mission
field in Peru. I was involved in a car accident and needed shoulder surgery. The real estate market collapsed and we
couldn't sell our house. We had endless troubles with a missions organization we thought was helping us. The girls and I
argued about many things that seem inconsequential now. We
were tired, and it was really stressful.

My friend said with genuine feeling, "Wow! That's an awesome honor! What a compliment!"

I always thought he was a little nuts.

He saw my expression and clarified, "Steve, you have actually picked a street fight with the Devil. Don't you know that?
This is a real spiritual battle, and you have chosen sides by taking to the field in active combat. You are not just going for the
Lord, you are moving against the enemy. Satan must really be
concerned to focus on you like that, huh? He must really not
want you to go."

I'd never thought of it that way. If you are sitting on the
sidelines of Christian life, not even looking for your God-given

mission, you can probably expect to be fat, dumb, and happy. However, if you decide to use your gifts and engage, get ready baby. The "dark side" will throw fiery darts of doubt and resistance at you. I can assure you from personal experience it is quite real and takes on many forms. Unexplainable things may happen to hobble and discourage you. You will feel afraid and unworthy. Don't buy it. Everywhere you see resistance, recognize where it comes from and respond. Pray it away in Jesus' name. Confess it, repent of it, and move past it. Stay focused and do your work, step by step, each day.

We are at war, and the enemy does not want you to therefore, go anywhere in the name of Jesus. Go anyway. Walk boldly. You'll be blessed beyond your dreams, and it will drive the Devil crazy! ❧

"For our struggle is not against flesh and blood, but ... against the powers of this dark world."

—Ephesians 6:12

The Sniper's Prayer

Saving Private Ryan – Combination of Psalms 22:11, 144:1-2, 25:2

"Be not that far from me, for trouble is near; haste Thee to help me. Blessed be the Lord my strength, which teacheth my hands to war, and my fingers to fight. My goodness, and my fortress; my high tower, and my deliverer; my shield, and he in whom I trust; who subdueth my people under me. O my God, I trust in thee: let me not be ashamed, let not mine enemies triumph over me."

—Recited by Private Jackson just before he was blown to smithereens.

86

THE END IN MIND

"If you want to reach a goal, you must 'see the reaching' in your own mind before you actually arrive at your goal."

—Zig Ziglar

IMAGINE WHAT YOU WANT your obituary to say when you die. It will sum up your whole life story in a few lines. Most people sipping coffee in their pajamas will grab a glimpse of it in the Sunday paper on their way to the sports section. It won't be important to the masses after you're gone. So why not make it important to you right now?

Think of it as drawing the construction plans for the house in which you always wanted to live. Sort of like taking a trip into the future so you can imagine what your present must look like. Does that sound crazy?

"Sh- Show me all the blueprints, Odie. Show me all the blueprints ... "

—Howard Hughes - The Aviator

Imagine, prayerfully dream, and write it down. You are the director of your own movie. You must know the end before it happens. Consider your obituary a basic script. Who do you want to be for the rest of your life? What role do you want to play?

Will your obituary say you made some money, bought a big home, had a cool car, took your family on a few trips, and died on the golf course? There's nothing horribly wrong with that, I guess, but is that the mark you plan to make and the "masterpiece" you're trying to build. Is that really the story you'll leave behind which will encompass the life God gave you? Is that truly your legacy?

If you actually sit down and write your obituary today with cool, noble, honorable, and adventurous things in it—things you hope God did in and through you during your life, not only will it help you imagine what you want to do with your time, talent, and treasure on earth, but you will get to spend the rest of your days trying to use your life in the selfless and noble ways you deliberately envisioned.

So sit down, write, and remember: It is impossible to do anything, even walk down the street, unless first you imagine yourself doing it. Then relax and watch what God does with your plans.

He will make your life a Masterpiece. ❧

"Imagine yourself as a living house. God comes in to rebuild that house.... You thought you were going to be made into a decent little cottage: but He is building a palace. He intends to come and live in it Himself."

—C. S. Lewis

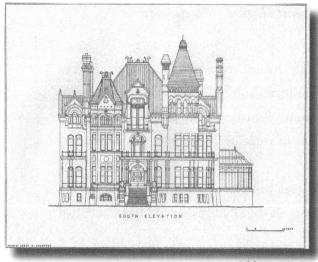

SOUTH ELEVATION

87

LET'S HAVE A CUP

T HE FACT IS, IF YOU GET OVER YOUR EXCUSES and get involved with missions, it is you who stands to benefit the most from the exchange. There's a poem I recite to my family every Christmas. Although they enjoy it, it's not so much for them as it is for me. This timeless verse helps me remember to stop being such a stick-in-the-mud and stop resisting God when He calls me to a mission. It is simple but powerful, and don't tell anyone, but I cry every time I read it:

A Cup of Christmas Tea

The log was in the fireplace, all spiced and set to burn.
At last the yearly Christmas race was in the clubhouse turn.
The cards were in the mail, all the gifts beneath the tree
And 30 days reprieve till VISA could catch up with me.

Though smug satisfaction seemed the order of the day,
Something still was nagging me and would not go away.
A week before, I got a letter from my old great Aunt.
It read: "Of course I'll understand completely if you can't,
But if you find you have some time how wonderful if we
Could have a little chat and share a cup of Christmas tea."

She'd had a mild stroke that year which crippled her left side.
Though house bound now my folks had said it hadn't hurt her pride.
They said: "She'd love to see you. What a nice thing it would be

For you to go and maybe have a cup of Christmas tea."

But boy! I didn't want to go. Oh, what a bitter pill
To see an old relation and how far she'd gone downhill.
I remembered her as vigorous, as funny and as bright
I remembered Christmas Eves when she regaled us half the night.
I didn't want to risk all that. I didn't want the pain.
I didn't need to be depressed. I didn't need the strain.
And what about my brother? Why not him? She's his aunt, too!
I thought I had it justified, but then before I knew
The reasons not to go I so painstakingly had built
Were cracking wide and crumbling in an acid rain of guilt.

—Tom Hegg

The poem goes on to say that the guy reluctantly goes to see his old great-aunt. He thinks he's doing it for her, but he's the big winner.

Has there ever been a time when you didn't want to hassle with helping someone, but after you did it was you who felt better? Do I even need to ask? ❧

"Heavenly Father, please guide us, protect us, and keep us ever mindful of the needs of others. In Jesus' name we pray, amen."
—learned from Lebo McLaughlin at Camp Maxwelton,
Rockbridge Baths, Virginia

PASSAGE VI
BUBBLING OVER

A "Hail Mary" Pass to Win the Bigger Vision

"My boy, you must strike while the iron is hot."

—my uncle, Arthur H. Berndtson, U.S. Navy captain and
recipient of the Silver Star

88

A HEROIC QUEST

"Look Christ in the face—whose mercy you have professed to obey—and tell Him whether you will join heart and soul and body and circumstances in the march to publish His mercy to the world."

—William Booth, founder of the Salvation Army

ERVING THE LORD on this urgent mission to earth makes my daily life much bigger than me. I am therefore happier and more fulfilled on a regular basis. Without God and the bigger role I get to play on His stage, life is flat and boring to me. Without Him, I have no true, enduring purpose.

Missionary service feeds my self-esteem and makes me feel like I'm in a heroic play every day. Have you ever read Don Quixote by Miguel De Cervantes Saavedra? This classic is about a man who charges boldly forward on a quest for all those good and honorable things he feels deeply about, whether they make logical sense to others or not. A walk in Christian missions is much like this.

To dream the impossible dream
To fight the unbeatable foe
To bear with unbearable sorrow
To run where the brave dare not go
To right the unrightable wrong
To love pure and chaste from afar

To try when your arms are too weary
To reach the unreachable star

This is my quest, to follow that star
No matter how hopeless, no matter how far
To fight for the right, without question or pause
To be willing to march into Hell for a Heavenly cause

And I know if I'll only be true, to this glorious quest,
That my heart will lie peaceful and calm,
When I'm laid to my rest
And the world will be better for this:
That one man, scorned and covered with scars,
Still strove, with his last ounce of courage,
To reach the unreachable star.

—Joe Darion, "The Impossible Dream," from the musical
Man of La Mancha

Do yourself a favor and step into a larger story. It doesn't matter what it is or where it is. The mission of service will make you feel great! Sometimes we are deceived into believing that we are small, and that our lives don't mean much in the grand scheme of things. We go about our day-to-day chores with a feeling of futility and meaninglessness. This couldn't be further from the truth. You were made "in His image" my friend. Your mission is of the highest importance. You were not placed here simply to eat, sleep, work and play.

Find your rightful, God-given role on the grand stage, and discover the most profound and satisfying happiness of your life.

Instinctively, you already know what it is. ❧

"When our daily actions fulfill a bigger purpose, the most powerful and enduring happiness can happen."

—Gary Keller – Founder of Keller Williams Realty

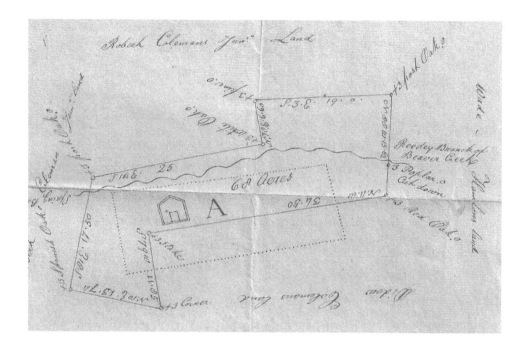

89

THE WEST WALL

"Not so far from here there's a very lively atmosphere,
everybody's goin' there this year
and there's a reason, the season never closes there
love and music you'll find everywhere
people always having fun down there, so come along."

—Desi Arnaz, "C-U-B-A"

I WAS BORN A COUPLE OF MONTHS after the Cuban revolution in 1959, and all my life I have been told Cubans are bad, and that the country is a dark, evil place full of Russian spies, communist cutthroats, and hateful, bloodthirsty, liars in general. This country was so horrid that Americans couldn't even go there most of my life. My upbringing told me Cubans were not to be trusted, and I believed it. Years later, Al Pacino in Scarface didn't help my perceptions about this Caribbean neighbor, with lines like, "You wanna play rough? Okay. Say hello to my little friend!"

Our family was once in a Lima, Peru, bus station on our way to find a boy who had disappeared from one of our orphanages. (You'll have to read about The Highwayman another time.) I met a pastor from the Cayman Islands in that bus terminal who encouraged me to begin missions to Cuba. I prayed about it, doors opened, and I took two teams there in 2012. I must admit, I was afraid when we landed the first time. All those scary perceptions rose to greet me when I approached customs and immigration at José Martí International Airport in Havana.

Do you know what I found in Havana? Cheerful, loving people who reminded me of why I had always suspected I would be drawn to Cuba: the I Love Lucy television show. The music, deep laugh and childlike spirit of Ricky Ricardo had been my only positive introduction to this otherwise cursed, taboo island. This joyful character played by Cuban-born Desi Arnaz is alive and well in Cuba today. Parts of Old Havana remind me of New Orleans with artists, amazing food, and beautiful music pouring out of ancient buildings into the streets. These wonderful people are every bit as much our kindred neighbors as anyone in the world. They're right next door, and they need us and the love of Christ in a big way.

"This is the most beautiful land one has ever seen."
—Christopher Columbus, arriving in Cuba in 1492

The fifty-five year-old, Cold War economic embargo the USA has maintained against Cuba began to soften in 2011. I am so thankful to our government for this opportunity to lead missions there and will enjoy our complete freedom there. It's not only a chance to build God's Kingdom in the fledgling churches there, but it's an opportunity to rebuild the relationship with this estranged neighbor who was once our friend. I am proud to be an ambassador, for God and country, to our

brother Cuba. I hope you will join me, because no one can influence another with a wall between them. It's time to build bridges and mend hearts. ❧

"Insanity: doing the same thing over and over again and expecting different results."
—Albert Einstein

Mr. Gorbachev, tear down this wall!'"
—President Ronald Reagan,

90

FOR GOD AND COUNTRY

FOR SUCH A TIME as this ...

It takes only a quick look around the United States of America right now to realize this once proud and blessed Christian country is now sliding away from the Lord, who gave us everything. It is because we have everything that many have been distracted and forgotten why we have it and who blessed us with it. As we gradually lose the Lord Jesus Christ in the daily life of our country, we also lose His mighty blessings upon us, day by day, bit by bit.

Katharine Lee Bates's lyrics to "America the Beautiful" say, "America, America, God shed His grace on thee." But how long is God going to keep sharing grace with us if we keep stripping Him from our country and daily life?

"If we ever forget that we are one nation under God, then we will be a nation gone under."

—President Ronald Reagan

Don't look now, friends, but the great ship is clearly listing. You can see it all around you. If we don't do something about it, I am afraid it will, with a little more time, slip beneath the proverbial waves. Then they'll be writing other songs about us.

Oh, they built the ship Titanic, to sail the ocean blue.
For they thought it was a ship that the water would never go through.

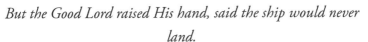

*But the Good Lord raised His hand, said the ship would never
land.
It was sad when that great ship went down.
Oh the heroes saved the weak, as the ship began to leak,
And the band on the deck played on.
With, "Nearer My God to Thee," they were swept into the sea.
It was sad when that great ship went down.*

—"The Titanic" William and Versey Smith

I truly believe the USA, land of the free and home of the brave, is in trouble. If we don't get off our pews and become proactive about getting God front and center, where He belongs in our national lives and in the lives of our children, then we are partially to blame when He walks away completely. Read your Bible, He's done it to people and "great" nations before.

Missions involvement, in whatever form you choose, is proactive and makes God smile. It energizes people and congregations. It is not just about caring for orphans or feeding the homeless or building a church. It is about actively sharing the Lord Jesus Christ with others and getting their attention for His message of salvation. Doing that not only impacts the people we reach out to, it impacts us and sets an example for our kids, our neighbors, and our world.

Today, you are here. You have many unique and valuable gifts. How are you being called to use them for the Kingdom?

*"For if you remain silent at this time, relief and deliverance for
the Jews will arise from another place, but you and your father's
family will perish. And who knows but that you have come to
your royal position for such a time as this?"*

—Esther 4:14

91

THE MOST SECRET PASSAGE

"Father, thank You for our ability to pull wisdom from Your Word, written thousands of years ago, to apply to our lives today."

—Pastor Greg Wallace

WHY WOULDN'T ANYONE at least be curious to read the Bible? For hundreds of years it was banned from the public. You could have been violently killed or imprisoned just for having one, but millions have taken the risk and still do today. Doesn't it make you wonder what's so powerful inside this book that people would literally make war and risk their lives over it?

The Bible is the ultimate secret passage!

Martin Luther translated the Bible into German, the language of the common people, and the Catholic Church wanted to have him killed for "letting this cat out of the bag." What's up with that? Luther said, "The Bible is the cradle wherein Christ is laid."

This book is transformational. The minute you start reading the Bible, the Lord will begin to communicate directly with you and transform your mind. It is the only place where you can truly find and develop a deep personal relationship with Jesus Christ. God will begin to reveal and confirm His mission for you on this earth through His Word. That's why they call it the "Living Word."

It's Alive. ❧

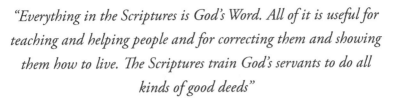

"Everything in the Scriptures is God's Word. All of it is useful for teaching and helping people and for correcting them and showing them how to live. The Scriptures train God's servants to do all kinds of good deeds"

—2 Timothy 3:16-17, cev

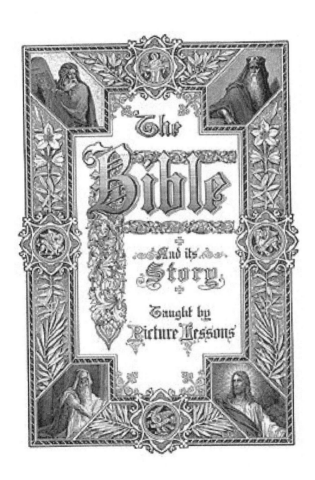

92

CLOSE THE BOX

I HAVE AN OLD FRIEND from England who regularly uses the phrase "at the end of the day" to begin his sentences. He is always trying to put "in a nutshell" what lesson has been learned or what goals we hope to achieve. For instance, "At the end of the day, there is no substitute for hard work." Or, "At the end of the day, it's just not good to drink and drive." Or maybe, "At the end of the day, we'll be glad we spent more time with our families."

One day, friends, it will be the end of the day for each of us here on earth.

I once heard a message on the radio from Dr. Tony Evans. (I love that guy! He makes it so real.) Tony was talking about how much he liked playing the game Monopoly. In the process of cutting deals and monopolizing all the property, he would gleefully trample every player on the board. His least favorite part was when the game was over, the pieces were picked up, and they "closed the box." After that, it really didn't matter much who won or lost. The game was over. No matter how intense the game got, at some point they finished, and in a short time it was forgotten. At the end of the day, Tony says, "They're going to close the box on you."

At the end of the day, your Monopoly game here will be over, and with the passing of a relatively short time, you will be forgotten forever. However, since you are here just visiting, what does it really matter?

Doesn't it make sense to use your time, talent, treasure, energy, passion, and purpose to carry out your Father's mission while you're here a short while? I think it is the best investment one can make, and the best insurance policy available. It's also a lot of fun.

Make it cool. Make it yours. You are unbelieveably blessed.❧

"You are not an accident. Your parents may not have planned you, but God did. He wanted you alive and created you for a purpose. You were made by God and for God, and until you understand that, life will never make sense. Only in God do we discover our origin, our identity, our meaning, our purpose, our significance and our destiny."

—Dr. Rick Warren, *The Purpose Driven Life*

92 & 2 Cents More

KINDNESS

WHEN IT COMES RIGHT down to it, in its most basic form, missionary service is simply kindness in the name of Christ. Helping people in need is the right thing to do. We have opportunities to serve others everyday, and yet we often pass them by. I wish we didn't.

Awhile back I was rummaging around in a used bookstore and came across *Reminisces of Happy Times* by Robert Wiley. Inside was a story called, "The Lifestyle of a Street Man." Several versions of this tale have been circulated on the Internet, and none I have encountered identify the original author. Since Mr. Wiley's book is a collection of pieces, compiled from many places, it is clearly not the original source of this story. He has my thanks for bringing it into public awareness. Beyond that, I have no idea where this story came from. It's a mystery.

Nonetheless, it needs to be told...

The Lifestyle of a Street Man
Author Unknown

One day a woman was walking down the street when she spied a beggar sitting on the corner. The man was elderly, unshaven, and ragged. As he sat there, pedestrians walked by him giving him dirty looks. They clearly wanted nothing to do with him because of who he was -- a dirty, homeless man. But when she saw him, the woman was moved to compassion.

It was very cold that day and the man had his tattered coat -- more like an old suit coat rather than a warm coat -- wrapped around him. She stopped and looked down. "Sir?" she asked. "Are you all right?"

The man slowly looked up. This was a woman clearly accustomed to the finer things of life. Her coat was new. She looked like that she had never missed a meal in her life. His first thought was that she wanted to make fun of him, like so many others had done before. "Leave me alone," he growled.

To his amazement, the woman continued standing. She was smiling -- her even white teeth displayed in dazzling rows. "Are you hungry?" she asked.

"No," he answered sarcastically. "I've just come from dining with the president. Now go away."

The woman's smile became even broader. Suddenly the man felt a gentle hand under his arm. "What are you doing, lady?" the man asked angrily. "I said to leave me alone."

Just then a policeman came up. "Is there any problem, ma'am?" he asked.

"No problem here, officer," the woman answered. "I'm just trying to get this man to his feet. Will you help me?"

The officer scratched his head. "That's old Jack. He's been a fixture around here for a couple of years. What do you want with him?"

"See that cafeteria over there?" she asked. "I'm going to get him something to eat and get him out of the cold for awhile."

"Are you crazy, lady?" the homeless man resisted. "I don't want to go in there!" Then he felt strong hands grab his other arm and lift him up. "Let me go, officer. I didn't do anything."

"This is a good deal for you, Jack," the officer answered. "Don't blow it."

Finally, and with some difficulty, the woman and the police officer got Jack into the cafeteria and sat him at a table in a remote corner. It was the middle of the morning, so most of the breakfast crowd had already left and the lunch bunch had not yet arrived. The manager strode across the cafeteria and stood by the table. "What's going on here, officer?" he asked. "What is all this? Is this man in trouble?"

"The lady brought this man in here to be fed," the policeman answered.

"Not in here!" the manager replied angrily. "Having a person like that here is bad for business."

Old Jack smiled a toothless grin. "See, lady. I told you so. Now if you'll let me go. I didn't want to come here in the first place."

The woman turned to the cafeteria manager and smiled. "Sir, are you familiar with Eddy and Associates, the banking firm down the street?"

"Of course I am," the manager answered impatiently. "They hold their weekly meetings in one of my banquet rooms."

"And do you make a good profit from providing food at the weekly meetings?"

"What business is that of yours?"

"I, sir, am Penelope Eddy, President and CEO of the company."

"Oh."

The woman smiled again. "I thought that might make a difference." She glanced at the cop who was busy stifling a giggle. "Would you like to join us in a cup of coffee and a meal, officer?"

"No thanks, ma'am," the officer replied. "I'm on duty."

"Then, perhaps, a cup of coffee to go?"

"Yes, ma'am. That would be very nice."

The cafeteria manager turned on his heel. "I'll get your coffee for you right away, officer."

The officer watched him walk away. "You certainly put him in his place," he said.

"That was not my intent. Believe it or not, I have a reason for all this." She sat down at the table across from her amazed dinner guest. She stared at him intently. "Jack, do you remember me?"

Old Jack searched her face with his old, rheumy eyes "I think so -- I mean you do look familiar."

"I'm a little older perhaps," she said. "Maybe I've even filled out more than in my younger days when you worked here, and I came through that very door, cold and hungry."

"Ma'am?" the officer said questioningly. He couldn't believe that such a magnificently turned out woman could ever have been hungry.

"I was just out of college," the woman began. "I had come to the city looking for a job, but I couldn't find anything. Finally I was down to my last few cents and had been kicked out of my apartment. I walked the streets for days. It was February and I was cold and nearly starving. I saw this place and walked in on the off chance that I could get something to eat."

Jack lit up with a smile. "Now I remember," he said. "I was behind the serving counter. You came up and asked me if you could work for something to eat. I said that it was against company policy."

"I know," the woman continued. "Then you made me the biggest roast beef sandwich that I had ever seen, gave me a cup of coffee, and told me to go over to a corner table and enjoy it. I was afraid that you would get into trouble. Then, when I looked over, I saw you put the price of my food in the cash register. I knew then that everything would be all right."

"So you started your own business?" Old Jack said.

"I got a job that very afternoon. I worked my way up. Eventually I started my own business that, with the help of God, prospered." She opened her purse and pulled out a business card. "When you are finished here, I want you to pay a visit to a Mr. Lyons. He's the personnel director of my company. I'll go talk to him now and I'm certain he'll find something for you to do around the office." She smiled. "I think he might even find the funds to give you a little advance so that you can buy some clothes and get a place to live until you get on your feet And if you ever need anything, my door is always opened to you."

There were tears in the old man's eyes. "How can I ever thank you," he said.

"Don't thank me," the woman answered. "To God goes the glory. Thank Jesus. He led me to you."

Outside the cafeteria, the officer and the woman paused at the entrance before going their separate ways. "Thank you for all your help, officer," she said.

"On the contrary, Ms. Eddy," he answered. "Thank you. I saw a miracle today, something that I will never forget. And thank you for the coffee."

She frowned. "I forgot to ask you whether you used cream or sugar. That's black."

The officer looked at the steaming cup of coffee in his hand. "Yes, I do take cream and sugar -- perhaps more sugar than is good for me." He patted his ample stomach.

"I'm sorry," she said.

"I don't need it now," he replied smiling. "I've got the feeling that this coffee you bought me is going to taste as sweet as sugar." ❧

ABOUT STEVIE

STEPHEN W. DYER has been a slow-learning sinner who often plays by his own rules. He was biblically illiterate, rarely went to church until he was 37, and like Jonah, ran away from the Lord to places most people have never even heard of. Now he guides and facilitates amazing international missions and is a mentor to the guys on the back row of your church. Stevie is a captivating public speaker, who incorporates his unique blend of world travels, missionary service and storytelling to encourage and motivate people off the bench and out on the field. He is forever asking the question: What's your mission?

A collector of antique navigation tools and weaponry, unique crosses, old photographs, rocks, seashells, pocketknives, unusual boxes, vintage books, keys, maps, and other stuff, Stevie admits to being a hoarder of international junk. His wife, Sheri, will not argue with that. They have two daughters, Ellie and Martha Anne.

Stevie envisions developing Missions Base Camp, a cool new kind of missionary academy and conference/retreat center. It will have fascinating workshops with the most accomplished and forward thinking instructors of our time, and serve as a place to develop advanced discussions, publishing, film production, and mission strategy. It will also be a home for retiring-teaching missionaries, and those resting from their work. Base Camp will be so inspiring and unusual, that even the biggest skeptic will be curious.

Dyer Family Missions is located in Houston, Texas

SO WHAT'S YOUR STORY?

I would love to hear what you have to say. Part of the fun of writing is getting people's reactions, and I would like to know what you think about this book.

I especially want to hear your stories. How has the Lord been guiding you into missions? What's happened in your life that makes you dig, search, and dream about the Lord and your mission? How is God using unusual people, places, and circumstances to get your attention and get you going?

If you'd like to share, email me between one and three pages. Make it cool. Make it yours.

Be blessed,

Steve

713-628-1610

Stevie3249@gmail.com

www.DyerFamilyMissions.com

"Promise Me you'll always remember you're braver than you believe, stronger than you seem, and smarter than you think."

—A. Milne - Winnie the Pooh

SUPPORT OUR CHILDREN'S MINISTRY!
Commission to Every Nation
(Indicate gift is for Dyer Family)
P.O. Box 291307
Kerrville, Texas 78029-1307
For information call: 830-896-8326
DONATE ONLINE AT:
www.DyerFamilyMissions.com

For additional copies of

SECRET PASSAGES
OF
STEVIE THE GUIDE

How
Ordinary People
DISCOVER
An Extraordinary Life
(*no matter where You came from*)

$19.95

visit DyerFamilyMissions.com
email Stevie3249@gmail.com
or call 713-628-1610
@StevieTheGuide (tweet this)

Quantity discounts are available.

Austin Brothers Publishing
817-366-9924
wterrya@gmail.com
www.AustinBrothersPublishing.com

CPSIA information can be obtained at www.ICGtesting.com
Printed in the USA
LVOW03s0242160814

399445LV00002B/3/P